DUNGEON
OF
DESPAIR

By The Same Author

TEARS AND SCARS

DUNGEON
OF
DESPAIR

PENJENI MADZIKANGAVA

Harp bookz International
An Imprint of TatendaCharlesMunyuki Publishing

DUNGEON OF DESPAIR

First published in Zimbabwe in 2016
Harp Bookz International
an imprint of Tatenda Charles Munyuki Publishing

Copyright © Penjeni Madzikangava 2016
Cover Illustration Copyright© Straightline Designz 2016
Cover illustration by Straightline Designz 2016

ISBN   978 0 7974 7251 8

Printed and bound by Harp Bookz International,
Harare, Zimbabwe.
harpbookz@gmail.com

facebook.com/tcmpublishingzim

CHAPTER 1

THE BREAKTHROUGH

Three days later, Amai was released after paying an admission of guilty fine. Fortunately, things started to look rosier for the family. Mudhara got a job with the Williams in Fern Valley as a cook.

A few weeks later, he came for Bhudhi Rotario, the Chidhumutumu expert whom he had found a job as a gardener for the Williams. Bhudhi Rotario had just been married then.

How had he wormed his way out of the *gota*, the traditional boys' bedroom? That brother of mine was rather quiet and shy.

I still wonder how he got to strum the Chidhumutumu before inquisitive eyes at Society Parties. Chidhumutumu is an African drum popularised by the Korekores of Dande. The drum is fixed with a twine that runs through a hole at the centre. When pulled, the drum produces a unique sound that resonates and blends with other musical instruments. He was just but a reserved person who was always quick to retreat into his shell whenever provoked. He never flirted around like what boys of his age did.

He was different from the other brothers of mine Bhudhi Mairosi and Maikoro who would sneak into the traditional girls' bedroom, *nhanga* whenever our nieces from Hartley paid us visits. I was told the duo had devised means and ways of how they would hook up with our nieces Sitesiwero and Sitejimoo who would sleep and share blankets with our sisters. In there, Bhudhi Maikoro and Bhudhi Mairosi would make incestuous love to Sitejimoo and Sitesiwero.

They would sometimes alternate the sisters in their sexpades. I now know why these nieces of ours would always die to visit our homestead every school holiday.

I now know the reason behind my brothers' unholy alliances. They both had some badly decomposing closely guarded secrets that reeked in their closets. I now understand why Bhudhi Maikoro would gladly volunteer to offer his chickens up for slaughter whenever our nieces darkened our doors. I now know why my brothers and our two nieces would always get involved in some steamy or romantic suggestive physical contacts all in the name of *chiramu*.

I remember Mudhara preparing my elder brothers for marriage.

He would constantly remind them not to tie themselves down into a union before they would have bought themselves a she goat, a cow, a suit, a bicycle, a wristwatch obviously the Oris type, some blankets, a bed and a wardrobe.

But was that not asking for too much? Maybe that was the sole reason why Bhudhi Mairosi, the foul-mouthed and uncouthed one had one evening challenged Mudhara to reveal how much he had paid for Amai's lobola.

As if that was not enough, Bhudhi Mairosi who appeared to have had one too many, had asked Mudhara why he had married Amai before he had attained a quarter of the very targets he had set for us.

Bhudhi Mairosi had made it crystal clear that he would not take Mudhara's targets seriously because he was not qualified to lecture us on the virtues of life as he had dismally failed to steer the family ship to shores.

Bhudhi Mairosi had not minced his words when he disgorged that Mudhara had no mandate or business to lecture us on success as he was worse off than a vagabond.

The reason being he had in the past pig headedly and persistently refused to occupy council houses in the then Salisbury's Gillingham and Mutare's Dangamvura townships at a time when his homeboys were stampeding for the houses.

Babamunini Gorobheki and Amainini Jekunareta had managed to secure a house in Gillingham after they had formalised their marriage. Houses in the locations could only be availed or allocated to couples upon production of a marriage certificate thus the houses were referred to as *dzimba or mhatso dzemuchato.*

Most black men were against the solemnising of their unions especially at the conventional courts.

They felt those marriage certificates empowered women as the documents would inhibit on men's traditional desire to cohabit with girlfriends or worse still to pick around a plethora of concubines.

Bhudhi Mairosi had added that had Mudhara not won a lump sum in a card playing game known then as *njuga* whose proceeds he had used to build our homestead as well as buying some beasts, he would have nothing to show for his lengthy stints in Salisbury and Umtali.

Amai had also weighed in with another lump sum from another betting syndicate known *as njore, which* was strictly for women especially those from Malawi and Zambia.

Bhudhi had labelled Mudhara a *muchoni*. Muchoni was a pejorative term used to describe failed migrants who would have left home in search of greener pastures, only to return empty handed and poorer.

That statement galvanised Mudhara to fly into a rage. That statement was the one that broke Mudhara's silence.

Bhudhi Mairosi's vitriol had taken him off balance. He was simply caught off guard. None of us had ever challenged him the way Bhudhi Mairosi had done. No wonder why Mudhara had lost his marbles.

Any father would have acted the way he did. He had to act to save face. He had to take a bold decision, a bold stance, a bold action to reign in some errant members of the family. Bhudhi Mairosi had taken his freedom of speech too far.

A line had to be drawn for any of us who might have been harbouring any ambitions of dressing down Mudhara before all and sundry. Bhudhi Mairosi's tail had to be nipped in the bud.

He needed to be reined in just in time before he strayed too far into the wilderness. Mudhara swiftly drew a smouldering log from the fire with which he struck Bhudhi Mairosi on the head sending his visibly drunken son plodding to the ground.

Frothing at the mouth, Mudhara followed the stunned Bhudhi Mairosi who then was bleeding profusely, landing a flurry of blows before Bhudhi Maikoro and Bhudhi Rotario restrained him.

Foaming with a hot temper, Mudhara had made it crystal clear that he would not allow any of us to reign over him and worse still to challenge his authority. He was in charge and would remain the one and only head of the family until the day his Maker would have called him. As if that was not enough, he also went on to accuse Amai of influencing us to rebel against his authority. To prove that he were serious, he went into the kitchen and spilled relish and sadza that was almost ready for our long awaited super supper. We slept on empty stomachs that day.

Bhudhi Mairosi was later attended to by Sisi Gaudhenziya who dressed his wounds with a concoction of salt and soot. That incident that saw Mudhara running the family with an iron fist also signalled the end of Bhudhi Mairosi's beer drinking binges.

Mudhara would not allow any of us to offer suggestions in any matters unless he had asked for our opinions. He had transformed from being an affable character who could allow us to be his drinking mates as well as dancing partners, into a fearsome dictator.

CHAPTER 2

THE TYRANT

He was no longer the smiley one, but rather the snarling one. He had become a monster who would not hesitate to crush any dissenting voices ruthlessly, after all he was never meant to be a Ruth, who was expected to be merciful, gracious and kind hearted.

To test our loyalty and discipline levels, he would occasionally bring out that issue on lobola. Deep down our hearts and far from the madding Mudhara, we would speak in hushed tones over the unattainable feat of his targets which Bhudhi Mairosi and Bhudhi Rotario believed were designed to scuttle their chances of getting married.

Sure that feat was unattainable given that most blacks then earned mediocre wages that reduced them to the level of slaves. Mudhara would argue during the men's court, *dare* that if one were to marry before acquiring any of these prerequisites of items, chances were very high that they would struggle to realise their dream of owning those assets.

When nature finally read the marriage act to Bhudhi Rotario, he had not yet accomplished a quarter of the targets Mudhara had set for us during our *dare* meetings. But in all fairness, Mudhara had deliberately raised the bar too high and practically unvaultable. I mean none among us then could vault over that target if it were in a vaulting contest.

Bhudhi Rotario had only managed to buy a bicycle and a wristwatch, status symbols then. He would occasionally flaunt his possessions in a community that held the acquisition of those assets in high esteem. He would ride his spick and span new baby into town occasionally glancing at his wristwatch that shone brightly under the sun as if in agreement with the powers that be of the Universe, the Almighty. That watch, an Oris brand, would also shine brightly under the moon like a firefly.

Bhudhi Rotario would pass through Sakubva's Henry Tiyayi's Photo Studio where he would have a number of shots taken. He would pose with a tube of adhesive glue or solution corruptly referred to as *shurushuru*, peeping from his trousers' side pocket for the single eyed box, the camera.

He would allow the photographer to take a close up snap of him in a plethora of positions. He would show off his priceless bow tie, a Chapewe cap; the kangaroo type, cross belts corrupted to *makurubhande*, a wristwatch and a bicycle to his folks in Dande, Mt Darwin.

What he would not do was to take along his homemade guitar and Chidhumutumu to the Studio so as to have a photograph of him taken.

He would not dare to have a photo shot of him taken whilst strumming the homemade guitar or Chidhumutumu for music then was regarded as a profession for those who would have failed to make it in life, *marombe*.

No lady worth her salt would stoop so low as to swear allegiance to the heart of a man who dabbled in music.

No serious in-laws would marry off their daughter to a musician. No community worth mentioning would want to be associated with musicians for they were deemed floppers in life. Music then was viewed as a part-time or pass-time of an occupation.

Nobody ever thought that music could sustain a community. Nobody then ever thought that music could one day turn into a big business creating a lot of employment.

Nobody then could dream of music being a major attraction in any country. Nobody then could ever have thought of music turning into an attractive Arts industry worth a standalone ministry. Nobody then ever dreamt of music becoming a multibillion money-spinning venture or industry. Nobody then ever envisaged music turning into a multi-sectorial industry that would lure tourists into any country. That was then and this is now.

CHAPTER 3

THE KISS

Our brothers could use photos to court girls through a third party, a go between, a *gwevedzi*. Back then, photographs were in black and white. Tan trousers, a cheaper form of jean trousers were fashionable then. They went down well with some high-heeled shoes mostly high cuts known then as *maburuka mumumango* or platform.

Checked shirts under the Sting label with matching sunglasses known then as *mabhimbo* or goggles were the in-thing. Girls then were referred to in the community lingo as *machukazi* or *machuni*.

Like I alluded to earlier on, Bhudhi Rotario's days in the *gota* were fast approaching the sale by date. Something had to be urgently done before the community could start talking.

Any young man perceived to be ripe for marriage had to find a lady for marriage to avoid being buried with a dead rat or maize cob.

The fear of being accompanied with a dead rat or maize cob would galvanize young men into casting their lustful eyes far and wide in search of machukazi.

Real machukazi, I mean the marriable type, were hard to come by. It would take a year or two of constant and incessant courting before a young man could be accepted. Young men could be richly rewarded for their endurance, consistency, persistence and perseverance. Those were virtues worth of any serious suitor.

During the courtship period, young men then would not make the grave mistake of trying to kiss, fondle boobs or bums of the girls of their desire.

That was taboo and abomination that could plunge any promising proposal into disarray if not into smithereens. Fondling and kissing were taboo outside the marriage institution. Even those who were married then were not highly skilled in foreplay and kissing like this generation.

Kissing then only meant lips lipping each other, lips just touching each other and in unison, the Judaic kiss. That one popularised by mapositori, apostolic sect members from the Johane Marange. Back then, we would watch and giggle with our mouths covered with our petite hands trying desperately to muffle those giggles.

Regardless of sex or relationship, Mapositori would kiss each other as a sign of greeting. That practice known in the mapositori parlance as *kukodzvana* has its roots in the Bible.

Mapositori then draped in their white garments would kiss each other three times in quick succession. The kisses were well timed, laconic, short and precise. They kissed whenever they met but the rate was pronounced on their Sabbath Day, a day they would be attired in their traditional garb. It was known and still is, as the Holy Kiss, which was opposed to the Judaic kiss of betrayal. That practice seemed to have taken a hard knock with the advent of independence in 1980. Nobody has come out publicly as to why the practice appeared to be dying a natural death.

Maybe the mapositori are no longer as sacred as they used to be. What they have managed to hang on to is the keeping of their goatee beard, baldheads, polygamy, their staff or the shepherd stick, white garbs and dangling diapers

Mapositori were looked down upon. They were despised as good for nothing fellows, fellows who hid their lustful eyes behind a religion.

Despite marrying a massive twenty-five wives who would bear them children by the gross, children they usually would lose count of, mapositori would still stray out of their matrimonial bedrooms.

What was it that they would be looking outside marriage that their twenty-five wives would have failed to provide, bedroom antics maybe?

They married underage girls. Even up to this day, they still marry underage girls. They got away with that culture of theirs. Nobody bothered to take a keen interest in their activities. Nobody was inquisitive, then nobody invaded their privacy.

Now they face resistance from a proliferation of organisations that strive on making a killing by purporting to be advancing the cause of the girl-child. Mapositori tested their teenage girls for virginity and those that would have failed were given away for a song to elderly men as wives.

Nobody could raise a finger against them. Nobody could chastise them for the practice. They lived in their own communities where they did as they pleased. Their communities appeared to be divorced away from the rest of the world

Now just like everybody else, they live in a global village that takes particular interest in matters that does not concern them.

A village from which villagers would rush with bucketfuls of water to save a neighbour's house engulfed by an inferno leaving theirs at the mercy of tongues of flames. A village whose occupants would mourn and wail more than the bereaved.

There were no prying eyes. Nobody minded their affairs. They would not send their offspring to school for they believed the education system would corrupt them. Male children were given academic preference over their female siblings.

They sent their children to school to enable them to read the Bible as well as writing letters. The polygamous mapositori fathers would *chase away* their teenage sons fearing that they would get involved in amorous affairs with their stepmothers most of who would be their age-mates. They were synonymous with a taste for real tea with bread spread with margarine. Now many legislations that seem to target mapositori have been enacted at the behest of women empowerment lobby groupings. What used to be nobody's business has all of a sudden become everybody's business. Whatever they do now is now of interest to everybody. What used to be their concern has suddenly become everybody's concern. Their practice of marrying-off teenage girls has drawn the ire of girl-child networks.

Their reluctance to seek medical treatment has been widely condemned by the authorities and those that advocate for children's rights. The authorities have realised the role of mapositori in the political matrix, political parties have realised the importance in the power of numbers.

Instead of giving them a hair dryer of a treatment whenever they stray out of step with the laws of the country, political parties are no longer taking swipes at them. Instead, they are courting them for a perpetual partnership.

Johane Marange alongside Johane Masowe eChishanu now rank as the most religiously followed indigenous churches with followers dotted across the globe. Johane Marange who are led by High Priest St Noah Taguta, now boosts of several primary schools and a state of the art college St Noah, arguably the best of its kind in Africa. The majority of teachers who ply their trades at these schools, are mapositori most of who graduated from several universities.

But what they have not done is to build clinics and hospitals. In that area, they have remained as conservative as they come. Their faith remains resolute, that faith has stood the test of time, very unshaken. Some of them stubbornly believe that hospitals and clinics will never stop death from robbing us of our beloved ones.

They might delay the Biblical promise, but will never derail it. At the end of the day, death will finally prevail over all and sundry.

St Noah Taguta remains probably the world's first black Saint alongside the likes of St Peter, St John, St Barnabas, St Michaels, St Faith, St Joseph, only to mention a few.

Chapter 4

The Seal of Approval

Kissing, passionate kissing, deep kissing or *French Kissing* that involved an exchange of salivary fluids, was viewed as un-African and a borrowed culture whose roots were rooted elsewhere.

It was also known as tongue-to-tongue. Girls kept the chastity vows even though some of them might have been involved in mock lovemaking sessions as they played house.

Those in love then and not yet married would amble or stroll away a metre apart to counter temptations. Distance then mattered. It kept them Holy and under lock and key. Distance kept them at bay.

Distance kept their libidos, if ever they had any, under surveillance and under check. Families took a keen and particular interest into families in which their sons and daughters would be vying to marry into or from.

Parents always preferred to have their sons and daughters marrying into reputable families. Parents from the community would fall onto each other dying to have their sons and daughters marrying into farming experts, reputable hunters, reputable drummers, well known traditional spiritual healers, renowned traditional dancers like jikinya dancers, renowned African thumb pianists, African flute players and the well-cultured. Fathers would tip their sons to marry into certain families and certain young women. This usually took place during *dare* meetings. Most fathers would prefer a situation in which their sons would marry off into their traditional and long-time family friends, *madzisahwira*.

By the same token, mothers would also advise their daughters to marry into certain families and certain young men. Those laid-back discussions usually took place in the traditional kitchens.

No parents would bless their sons and daughters' marriages into broken up families or worse still families whose names would have been dragged into sorceries, witchcraft and wizardry for they reckoned those social ills would be passed on onto those who carried those families' names.

Bhudhi Rotario had a tall order up his sleeves. Our parents had made it crystal clear that they would not accept a SaManyika for a daughter-in-law. SaManyikas hail from Zimbabwe's Eastern Province of Manicaland adhered for their penchant for the Queen's language.

It was taboo for the SaManyikas not to spice their speeches with English words. The majority of Zimbabwe's prominent business icons, academia and politicians attended schools in Manicaland like Hartzell High School; *Hatso*, St Augustine High School; *kwaTsambe* and Marist Brothers. Students worth their salt would strive to go through the educational mill of these institutions. Any institutions outside these were not worth to write home about. You would hear the SaManyikas bragging that, *'Kuti usizi kufunda paTsambe, Hatso kana Marist hauzi kuenda kuschool ba.'* To them, Tsambe, Hatso and Marist were the yardstick that was supposed to be used as a barometer to measure a student's academic prowess.

There was a standing rule in the family, a hard and fast one for that matter. A rule that would not be broken or bent. The family would only accept a daughter-in-law from Dande or anyone of Korekore extraction.

So when Bhudhi Rotario formally announced his decision to get married despite his failure to attain targets that had been set by Mudhara, he found himself between a hard rock and a deep sea.

Although he would have loved to marry a girl from some reputable families from Dande, most of those he had eyed during his stay in the area could have been married or worse still displaced by the Chimurenga war that was raging through the area like an inferno.

Given a choice, he would have loved to get married to Queen who was a daughter to Mudhara Joramufiri. Word that had reached Umtali then was that, Dande was inaccessible, as it had been cut out by the Second Chimurenga War.

Villagers from Chipiso, Chigango, Pfunyanguwo, Bandimba, Katarira, Karanda, Dotito, Kajokoto, Pachanza, Nyombwe, Chahwanda, had all been rounded and shepherded into protected villages, *mumakeep* under some auxiliary forces from the District Administrator.

There was no way Bhudhi Rotario could have braved the ravaging war by travelling to Mt Darwin whose roads were strewn and infested with land mines, just for the love of his childhood sweetheart Queen whom I was told was of blinding beauty.

Her chocolate skin was soft to the touch and dazzling to the eye. I was also told that her beauty could rival that of cherubic babies.

During the night, he would always brag about how beautiful his Queen was. Nobody dared to tell Bhudhi Rotario in the face that beauty was in the eyes of the beholder.

As frustrations of failing to land the signature of his Queen took its toll on Bhudhi Rotario, he took to the bottle. The bottle could only refer to kachasu or vhinyu.

It was illegal for blacks then to imbibe bottled alcohol like Castle Lager, Black Label or Lion. Having had one too many of the bottled vhinyu and kachasu, Bhudhi Rotario would cycle home in the death of the night.

His arrival would only be announced by barking dogs whose raucous barks would disturb the serenity of the night. He would head for the kitchen in his drunken stupor where his cold sadza would be waiting for him, spoiling for a sparing contest. After filling his dine, he would stagger into the boys' bedroom, where he would find us snoring away.

He would pull out a homemade stool, made himself comfortable, fish out his homemade guitar, which he would strum with such gusto and verve. He would strum and sing a composition that he would have composed for the dream Queen.

The sounds would blend and serenade with rhythmic unison. Bhudhis Mairosi and Maikoro would grumble and groan with displeasure that surprisingly would flow with the tune.

The tune of love. The tune of protest. The tune of frustration. The tune of maturity. The tune of freedom from the clutches of childhood. He would play until his eyes were heavy with sleep.

So shy was Bhudhi Rotario that he would not pluck up enough courage to approach a girl in a courtship contest. He would sometimes send a letter bursting to the seams with passionate pleas of love to whomever he would have fallen for, through a gwevedzi.

The chosen gem would hungrily feast on the letter with passionate eyes, rescan the letter with roaming eyes before using her darting tongue to inform the messenger to tell Bhudhi Rotario to deliver the message of love in person.

This would present Bhudhi Rotario with a number of challenges. He was shy to the extent of stammering whenever he was in the company of a lady, to the extent of falling shot of soiling his pants.

No wonder why he would spend most of his time in the company of single mothers, *mvana,* who would be out to make amends in their love lives. Most ladies could be mischievous.

Was it mischief that led ladies then to verify if indeed those men who would have sent go betweens meant what they would have said or they would only be out to embarrass them? Surely, why these ladies would play hard to get when they would have received the passionate message loud and clear, still baffles me?

Surely why would these ladies send for the men behind the message when most of them would agree to get married to someone they would have only seen on a snap or photograph. It was ironic that some of these ladies who would have overzealously spurned the hands of the men until they had delivered the love dosages in person, would fall for any man they would have been told of through word of mouth.

CHAPTER 5

FALLING IN LOVE WITH A PHANTOM

Someone from another space, someone they would have never met or worse dreamt of meeting. They would blindly fall in love with someone whose background could have been doctored, a soiled background that could have been spruced up in readiness for a marriage.

Surely any man who would have sent for the hand in marriage of a lady he had not seen, but whose character he would have learnt and got to appreciate through the exploits of a skilful matchmaker, should have been treated with contempt and scepticism.

Bhudhi Rotario sent word to Tete Rubhineti who stayed at a farming compound near Mazoe Citrus that he was looking for a lady to marry. A lady who was marriable.

He also sent with a registered envelope, a black and white snap of his from Henry Tiyayi's Photo Studio. The photo revealed his possessions, his worth. The photo depicted him riding his most prized possession, the bicycle.

In the photo, he looked like a barrister, like someone who had just been admitted into the Law Bar. He looked like a Shakespearean, like someone who lived somewhere along Downing Street in England. He appeared like an adopted Prince at Queen Elizabeth's Palace. He looked like a charming Prince somewhere far from the jungles of a British colony. His tailed jacket resembled that sported by the Jit supremo Mhosva Marasha better known in the music circles as Biggie Tembo.

The photo that told Bhudhi Rotario's story a thousand times, depicted him as a man who had been drugged with a colonial mentality. The photo presented him as a colonial caricature, a colonial symbol, a colonial statement, a colonial legacy.

Anything white then was held in high esteem and anything black then was looked down upon with distaste and disdain.

When the photo arrived at the compound, it did not take long before a beautiful teenage girl Rokadhiya fell head over heels in love with Bhudhi Rotario.

She had been hooked to the man on the photo picture, the

phantom. Rokadhiya was the most beautiful nineteen-year-old teenager in the compound, a compound belle.

Times without number, a number of young foremen had fought over her following some beer sprees. None of them had succeeded in winning her heart.

She had been drugged with heaps of praises that were drawn by her blinding beauty. She had vowed never to marry anyone from the compound. Who could blame her? She had seen her stocks rising by each passing day. Her beauty called for a better league of love, a better suitor, someone from a big city like Salisbury, Umtali, Bulawayo, Gwelo, Gatooma, Marandellas or Que Que. She preferred Salisbury where she would pit her exquisite looks with white ladies, *vana misisi.*

Rokadhiya believed that she had what it took to give white belles a good run for their monies despite them being blessed with their natural beauty that was complimented with long, pointed noses and long hair that resembled a white horse's mane.

She knew that her looks were the only ticket that could de-plunge her out of the murky waters of poverty. She knew that her fair looks could salvage her from circling vultures from her compound.

She believed her God-given looks could be her answer to a better life, far from the hustle and bustle of compound life where *Chilapalapa* and *Chibhende* form of communication were the in-thing.

Chilapalapa was a language coined by whites especially those of Boer extraction. The language that had a heavy Malawian and Zambian accent enabled white farmers to communicate with their illiterate workers mostly from Malawi and Zambia.

Chibhende was a cryptic language used by rival ghetto and compound youths who would be out to avoid detection. Only those who knew the password could decipher or encode those messages.

Rokadhiya detested Chilapalapa and Chibhende with a passion and was determined to extricate herself from the clutches of these two communication tools. She desperately needed to sleep on a spring bed, which she had last slept on as a child before she was expelled for bed-wetting.

She was sick and tired of sleeping on a makeshift bed made of discarded heavy empty tobacco sacks, *mavhanda.* She longed for a pillow on which she would shed tears of love. She hated using her palm for a pillow.

Every morning she would wake up with stretch marks streaking all over her face, imprints of the heavy sacks. She was tired of bathing without a cake of soap and a towel, *kugeza nembama* and *ruredzo*.

Ruredzo was a traditional herb found along some rocky river banks that produced foam when pounded by a stone. Due to the foam that it produced when pounded, poor families traditionally used it as a substitute for soap.

How Rokadhiya yearned for a husband who could spoil her. She longed for a husband who could extricate her family from the clutches of poverty, the *mukuwasha mukuyu* type who would be prepared to trade his first family for his second family. How she yearned to be de-flowered on a metal bed.

She longed to move to the city where she would not sleep in a grass thatched pole and dagga hut, but in a servant's quarters, which were roofed with some zinc sheets, or in the African townships whose houses were roofed with asbestos.

Rokadhiya longed to eat from breakable plates, breakable cups and breakable saucers. She yearned to have her hair plaited. She dreamt of heeling away in stiletto shoes, wheeling away her baby in a perambulator, *purema*.

She yearned for the spiced or Madras Curry taste of rice and chicken that she had tasted occasionally during Society Parties and during Christmas and New Years' holidays. She longed for a better diet for her looks deserved one.

She no longer wanted to share a maize cob with some mucus dripping elders who would dupe her saying, *'Ndipe chibage chako ndikuvhurire njanji inoenda kuSalisbury.'*

Rokadhiya dreamt of taking a bath in the company of her would-be husband in a bathroom that was adorned with a mirror. She was fed up of bathing in a *chinjausi* where some Peeping Toms would be lurking.

Her beauty deserved to be reflected in a real mirror not a makeshift one in which she would use water in a dish to mirror her image. Rokadhiya desperately wanted an urgent divorce from firewood and cow dung smoke that always left her eyes shedding tears of abject poverty. She longed to prepare her husband's food on a paraffin stove. She dreamt of dancing the foxtrot at a concert with her husband. She yearned to exchange pleasantries with white couples who she would have met at Bon Marche, OK Bazaar, TM

Supermarkets, Meikles Hotels, Jameson Hotels and Vistarama movie house for bioscope or at Drive Inns. What Rokadhiya seemed to have had forgotten was the fact that these places were out of bounce for blacks, herself included.

She yearned for some endless rides in some city buses that plied various routes. She yearned to rest her arm on the bus window.

She was sick and tired of seeing the kapitaus perched on the mudguards of tractors whilst she and her colleagues travelled rough in a crowded trailer at the farm. She no longer wanted to buy her own food for consumption.

CHAPTER 6

TRIBULATIONS OF A MATCHMAKER

Tete Rhubhineti, who was known for her singing prowess and fancy footwork on the dancefloor during Jit competitions held at the compound during full moons, was slowly curving herself a niche in the matchmaking industry.

She had done some moon lighting for several young men whose offers for marriages would have been spurned several times before. She had done that for a song, usually for an African bird and a bucketful of sorghum or millet. She had managed to convince a number of beautiful girls to get married to a number of kapitaus and maforomani.

That saw her getting some rises in her grades at work. A rise in grade would also mean a surge in wages, lighter duties, rations, some favours and better accommodation.

She would enjoy favours from couples she would have joined in marriages. Her stocks as a reputable matchmaker rose with each flirting day.

Whenever marital problems reared their ugly heads in households that she would have sweated over to put together, she would be called upon to trash out those problems. She had done that with distinction and honour.

Legend had it that all the marriages that she had matchmade, had managed to weather storms associated with marriages. They had simply withstood the test of time. Despite her being single, she seemed to proffer solutions to every marital problem. She was a living panacea to marital challenges that then haunted marriage institutions.

Being a matchmaker was never a stroll in the park. It had its pros and cons. A matchmaker would be held responsible for the breakup of a union they would have solemnised or sanctified by giving it a green light. The buck of a crumpled union would stop at the matchmaker.

Should a couple discover with the passage of time that they are not compatible, the blame would lie squarely on the matchmaker for having overlooked or worse, having doctored some traits.

Should a lady who would have eloped to a man known to the matchmaker or worse, whose background a matchmaker claimed to know a lot about, vanished off the face of the Earth, the matchmaker would be picked up by police for interrogations and possibly charged with kidnapping as an accomplice.

When Bhudhi Rotario's snap arrived at Tete Rhubhineti's place, she passed it on to three teenage girls whose personal reputations and family backgrounds she greatly admired. The trio were Rokadhiya, Roziwinda and Roffinna.

The three had been raised in the African tradition in which respect and chastity were the hallmark of a good African woman, a virtue every man would take pride in paying *mombe yechimanda*.

No man would want to be associated with a de-flowered woman, *gasva* or *gura* hence the Shona novel *Ndiani Acharima Gura?*

Any girl who would have lost her virginity in dubious circumstances, circumstances other than in a marriage setup, would put her family's name in bad light. Her mother and aunts would come in for some flaks. No man then would pay a bride price for a used woman, an unwrapped present.

This was the reason why girls then would elope with the guy who would have de-flowered them. No man worth his salt would stick to a woman whom he would have found defiled.

Questions about the number of men that girl would have bedded before meeting her current man, would always crop up.

And legend has it that chances of that girl cheating with those men whilst in a marriage, would be very high. The trio were girls who were respected in the society, considered well cultured and principled. They were considered fresh from the garden. Merry were their hearts for they were virgins.

Virginity was their most priced asset, their claim to fame. To them the price of their virginity could be equated to that of gems such as pearls, gold and diamonds. To them there was no price for loose biscuits.

They were not loose, but still intact with the seal of approval still sticky, unbroken and un-tempered with. The trio had not auctioned their virginity for a packet of the much hyped and praised Choice Assorted biscuits and a bottle of carbonated soft drink, like Coca Cola or Fanta.

They did not want to drag their families' good standing into the mud. To them love was not proven by being laid by any man.

They were not in a hurry to have intended benefits of their future husbands devoured by passers-by. Roffinna, Roziwinda and Rokadhiya sought to impress Tete Rhubhineti.

They would compete to cook for her, do her dishes, her laundry, assisted her with some household chores as well as tilling and harvesting her fields.

CHAPTER 7

PICTURE ON THE WALL

They too had been impressed by the gentleman they had seen in the photo. The trio competed to win the heart of the gentleman whose photo hung perilously on the dirty walls of Tete Rhubhineti's dhanduru.

They would smile past the gentleman in the photo whenever they passed through Tete Rhubhineti's place. The trio would salivate whenever they stared at the man in the photo.

They would love it whenever the gentleman in the photo stared back and reciprocated with a contagious smile, a killer smile. They would swing their bums and swing their unbrassiered breasts whose pointed nipples would bounce rhythmically with their gait. Breasts that no man had ever fondled.

They would stand akimbo before the gentleman in the photo, resting their dainty hands on their hips, hips that no man had ever massaged. They would stand there smiling slowly and sweetly at the gentleman in the photo, parading their kissable lips, lips that no man had ever kissed before.

They would gleefully show their teeth to the man whose picture hung on the wall; teeth, which they would have cleaned with ash or river, sand from a flowing river using their index fingers as a makeshift toothbrush, teeth they would have cleaned using a makeshift toothbrush from a bristled strip off a muchakata branch. They would wipe sweat off the gentleman in the photo. They would wipe dust off the shoes of the gentleman in the photo.

They would compete to wash clothes that belonged to the gentleman in the photo which they would hang out to dry on the wall where the gentleman in the photo would be watching from a vantage point.

They would compete to wipe off dust from the man on the photo's magogorosi, dust that would have accumulated as he wheeled past in a cycle track. They would compete to win favours from the man in the photo, to see who among them would be given a ride on the carrier of his bicycle.

They would compete to stretch their arms to the gentleman

whose picture hung on the wall. They would complain to be pampered with the gentleman whose picture hung on the wall.

They would compete for affection from the gentleman whose photo dangled on the wall. They would all lay claim and embrace with the love of the gentleman whose photo swung on the wall.

The triple Rs would spruce up their images just to impress the character behind the gentleman whose photo hung on the wall. They would apply Ambi and Ponds just to look gorgeous for the man whose picture hung on wall.

Tete Rhubhineti had promised them that it was only a matter of time before the gentleman on the photo came to price away one of them, the fortunate one. They would get involved in cat fights, fighting for the attention of the gentleman on the photo. The three would pour their hearts to the man on the photo, with regards to how Tete Rhubhineti would be unfairly treating them.

They would confide in the picture on the wall of how Tete Rhubhineti would be giving the other two an unfair advantage. They would share top secrets, family secrets with their confidante, the gentleman in the photo.

They would backstab each other all for the picture on the wall, all for love. They would swear allegiance to the man whose picture hung on the wall. They would vow to stick it out until death, with the man in the photo who in the figment of their own imagination, would nod in agreement.

They would imagine themselves strolling around the streets of Umtali arm in arm with the man of their dreams, the man in the photo.

They would vow to bear the gentleman in the photo children by the gross. They would vow to remain faithful to the picture on the wall. They would vow to satisfy sexually, the gentleman in the photo. They would compete to compliment the gentleman in the photo.

They would spite each other like women in a polygamous set up just to win the attention of their smiley soulmate, the gentleman in the photo. They would fantasise imploring the gentleman in the photo to switch off the lights before their steamy debut night.

They would fantasise begging the gentleman in the photo gently and gingerly going about his business of rapturing the seal of approval. They would imagine being ploughed into by the gentleman's ploughshare not on a rickety wooden rough bed, but a metal sturdy one, one that would wail as if in excruciating pain.

They would imagine wincing, groaning and moaning in piercing pain as the gentleman in the photo would be navigating his way into one of them.

They would imagine sinking their teeth into the broad and brawny hairy chest of the gentleman in the photo when the pain became unbearable leaving some indelible scars, love bites.

They would imagine the smiley gentleman's smile turning into a squawk of alarm as teeth sank into his flesh leaving trickles of oozing blood.

They would imagine walking with a limp the following morning after the gentleman in the photo would have accomplished his mission of negotiating his way into their treasure island.

Somewhere at a compound in Mazoe, their families would be ululating singing, *'Makorokoto wedu wadadisa, tichamutengera pata pata.'*

Deep down there in Mazoe, the clan would be waiting to dispatch their *munyai* or *sadombo*, the go-between for their pride price, *roora, makandinzwa naani, tsvagirai kuno, mbudzi dzemushonga, maputi, badza, mafukidza dumbu, mombe yehumai,* yechimanda nedanga.

CHAPTER 8

CASTING LOTS

When the time for the final selection finally came, Tete Rhubhineti had to go through a torrid time. The trio had impressed her so much that they had left a lasting impression. None of them had been found wanting in crucial areas, areas that mattered most.

The trio had fared well. A very thin line demarcated the trio's performances. They had not served their best for the last but had impressed from the first. The trio had rarely put any foot wrong.

Tete Rhubhineti had to sleep over for the best choice. She wanted the best wife for her brother's eldest son to set the bar high for his siblings. She did not want to be blamed by the entire clan should the marriage fail to work out. She did not want to cross paths with her temperamental brother, Mudhara. Tete Rhubhineti did not want to see her brother's family in turmoil because of a wayward daughter-in-law.

She did not want anybody to drive a wedge between Mudhara and her. She had to do her homework well. To her, failure was not an option. She finally resolved to consult a well-known traditional healer Sekuru Muroyiwehama famed for his supernatural powers. Legend had it that so powerful was Sekuru Muroyiwehama that he would perform traditional rites, *kuparura matare* whilst sitting on a cowhide that would be buoying on top of a river.

Legend had it that he possessed the largest snake in the compound, a snake that would move around other people's fields sweeping away crops. The compound was abuzz with news that Sekuru Muroyiwehama possessed some lightning manufacturing charms.

He was also in the habit of bedding unsuspecting women during their sleep using *mubobobo*, *gondwawaturuka* or *mukwarakwato*. The compound was awash with rumours that Sekuru Muroyiwehama was also in possession of a hyena and a vulture's head, which he used during consultations.

They said all his prophesies were spot on. All his prophesies would come to pass. Nobody from the compound dared to challenge him to a demonstration of power contest.

Nobody from the compound could dare to cross his labyrinth of paths. Nobody from the compound could dare to bear false witness against him neither could anybody dare to speak ill of him.

He was a no nonsense man, an untouchable as well as the undisputed king of charms who had cracked open a number of traditional mysteries.

When Tete Rhubhineti consulted him for his supernatural opinion on who Bhudhi Rotario should choose from the trio who were running neck-to-neck for the crown, Sekuru Muroyiwehama had to use lots, *hakata* to come up with the winner.

And the winner was Rokadhiya Mukoranebhande.

Tete Rhubhineti sent a telegram to Bhudhi Rotario notifying him of the latest news.

He in turn informed Amai and Mudhara of the good news. Mudhara gave Bhudhi Rotario the green light to travel to Mazoe for his jewel.

Before travelling to Mazoe, Bhudhi Rotario had to purchase a new suitcase, a number of new dresses for his wife-to-be Rokadhiya. He later informed Tete Rhubhineti of his plans to visit her place with the intention of eloping with Rokadhiya.

In turn, Tete Rhubhineti had confided in Rokadhiya who she had advised to prepare for her new life in Umtali, far from the madding compound dwellers.

The gods had finally smiled on her. She had finally won the heart of the gentleman whose picture hung elegantly on the wall.

She would be leaving behind her bitter rivals Roffinna and Roziwinda who she believed she had beaten hands down for the crown, the gentleman whose picture hung on the wall. She would become the first one from her clan to have broken free from the clutches of compound life.

She would be making history by becoming the first from her clan to have travelled and lived in the mountainous and scenic city of Umtali.

Bhudhi Rotario finally travelled to Mazoe for her queen. Tete Rhubhineti introduced him to the duo that had fallen by the wayside, Roffinna and Roziwinda after which she formally introduced him to the one who had won it for the compound, Rokadhiya.

Bhudhi Rotario appeared to have been charmed by the burly built Roffinna who was blessed with some big boobs, pillows and a commensurate curvaceous bottom, shock absorbers. Tete Rhubhineti poured cold water on Bhudhi Rotario's choice by confiding in him what Sekuru Muroyiwehama had said during consultations.

Sekuru Muroyiwehama's lots had revealed that Roffinna had unknowingly been initiated into witchcraft by her paternal grandmother who was feared for her nocturnal business.

Roffinna shed tears of disappointment, tears of despair, tears of frustration and tears of self-denial. The beautiful Roffinna cried on his shoulders, weeping to the gods. Together with Bhudhi Rotario, they cried hysterically drenching with warm feminine tears Bhudhi Rotario's t-shirt.

At the river between the compounds, Bhudhi Rotario had to summon all his consoling skills to contain the raging fire of tears of dejection, tears of rejection. He had to wipe away the cascading tears by the marauding, meandering, gurgling, frothing, salivating, weeping river whose mourning serenaded with some singing birds.

There by the flowing river that appeared to flow in protest against Roffinna's fate, Bhudhi Rotario's hands were allowed to grope, caress, stroke, cuddle and manoeuvre in sacred areas, areas that no man had ever been allowed to explore.

Bhudhi Rotario was allowed to plough deeper with his ploughshare into Roffinna's virgin land, land that had laid fallow since birth. Blood that signalled the rapture of the seal of approval flowed.

By the river, the waters had watered down Roffinna's frustrations, which appeared to be petering out as the day flirted by. Bhudhi Rotario had to endure pangs of excruciating pain as Roffinna involuntarily sunk her teeth into his strapping and hairy chest to leave indelible scars, love bites.

Bhudhi Rotario had danced into the whims of the rejected and well-figured young woman. He had passionately kissed, fondled and continued to slice into Roffinna who was then drugged with dosages of love from the gentleman whose photo still hung on Tete Rhubhineti's dimly lit wall, whose heart she hoped to win.

Roffinna had hoped for a change of heart, rescinding of a harsh decision, a decision that ironically had been arrived at by the gods of the land. The gods had spoken and Bhudhi Rotario was young and naïve to appeal against the gods' case, their will.

The gods must have been crazy for trying to deny Bhudhi Rotario a chance to marry his first choice, Roffinna. By the river, the duo had panted for gasps of breath under heavy gulps of kisses.

When darkness ghosted into the compound, enveloping the river under a gloomy cover of darkness, the two lovebirds trooped to the compound. At the periphery of the compound, they had kissed passionately under the cover of darkness before bidding each other farewell.

Bhudhi Rotario had vowed to go against the gods' will and advice by marrying Roffinna. He had promised to sleep over it. And slept over it, he surely did.

The following morning Bhudhi Rotario announced to Tete Rhubhineti his decision to marry Roffinna. Tete Rhubhineti advised Bhudhi Rotario on the dangers of throwing caution to the wind by going against the gods' recommendations.

She also advised Bhudhi Rotario on the dangers of marrying Roffinna whose paternal grandmother was notorious for dabbling in witchcraft. She was notorious for possessing zvishiri.

Legend has it that whenever a person who possesses zvishiri gives birth, the invisible birds will also give birth. The owner of the invisible birds would in turn distribute the birds to close relatives especially females.

When a girl who would have been blessed with a *chishiri*, the invisible bird, got married and gave birth, the chishiri would also give birth. That's how they multiplied. Whenever a chishiri was sent to strike a victim, it would leave the victim's mouth twisted as if the victim would have suffered a stroke.

The owner of zvishiri when angered could only save their victim from being struck with the invisible birds by consistently spitting on the ground during an altercation. This was what Tete Rhubhineti tried to tell Bhudhi Rotario but he could not take heed of any of that advice.

Having exhausted all her persuasive skills, Tete Rhubhineti gave up the struggle and threw the ball into Bhudhi Rotario's court. Tete Rhubhineti also feared for her safety from the marauding invisible birds.

Bhudhi Rotario having triumphed over Tete Rhubhineti and the gods, stood up and went to Roffinna's place to deliver the good news. He instructed Roffinna to pack her *katundu* as they were supposed to leave that night for Umtali.

Roffinna was ecstatic about the news. She took flight to the moon like an astronaut with that news. Her dream of finally moving to a city had come true. The gods of the land had finally answered her prayers.

CHAPTER 9

TABLES TURNING

She had finally turned the tables against Rokadhiya who the gods of the land had chosen over her and Roziwinda.

She would tell Sekuru Muroyiwehama off his face that he had manipulated results from the lots to settle for Rokadhiya who was the last and only daughter to his best friend Mudhara Mukoranebhande.

When dusk finally kissed the farm, a hive of activity ensued to signal the arrival of darkness. By the time darkness devoured the farm, Amaiguru Roffinna had already finished packing her katundu in a tattered and torn travelling bag that had seen better days.

She had clandestinely and stealthily tiptoed her way out of the family house and headed towards a huge Muhacha tree that grotesquely stood on the periphery of the farm. That huge Muhacha tree which was believed to have been a meeting place, a rendezvous for witches who plied their trade on the farm.

That Muhacha tree had become a rendezvous for Bhudhi Rotario and Amaiguru Roffinna during the short stint that Bhudhi Rotario had stayed on the farm.

When Roffinna arrived at their rendezvous, Bhudhi Rotario and Tete Rhubhineti were already there waiting in bated breath for her.

In no time, the trio were trudging along a beeline that connected to the main road. They panted, stumbled, huffed and puffed under the heavy luggage. Amaiguru Roffinna had not brought much of her clothes.

Tradition demanded that whenever a girl eloped, she would leave behind much of her clothes to her siblings. Her husband, the one she would have eloped with, would fill in the vacuum that she would have created in her wardrobe. That was a test. That tradition would test how caring the husband would be.

When the trio finally arrived at the main road that led to Salisbury, they heaved a huge sigh of relief. In no time, Bhudhi Rotario flagged down a sleek Peugeot 404 station wagon that belonged to a local headmaster, a Mr Mabharani.

After loading the heavy luggage into the car, it glided back into the road leaving Tete Rhubhineti waving side-splittingly at Bhudhi

Rotario and Amaiguru Roffinna. Mr Mabharani drove them to Salisbury's National Railways Station where they intended to board a train to Umtali.

Bhudhi Rotario lavished his sweetheart with food. Amaiguru Roffinna munched the food until her jaws ached. That night, she became almost a permanent visitor to the lavatory. She was under siege from a running stomach. Passengers in the coach in which she was booked with Bhudhi Rotario could hear her stomach rumbling from a distance.

Bhudhi Rotario could hear some giggles from other passengers who would murmur in hushed tones, '*Inzwa kurira kwenyoka dzavhunduka chirungu.*'

Bhudhi Rotario blamed himself for lumping Amaiguru Roffinna with alien food. Amaiguru Roffinna who was held spellbound by what she had seen in the train, kept Bhudhi Rotario under siege with a myriad of questions.

Only a few that were sensible demanded answers, but the rest were rhetoric and naïve to be polite. She was delighted as well as bemused by the lights that flooded the coach.

She could not imagine how whites had tamed and harnessed several full moons, which they had tied into the coach. She reckoned that the white men's moons were more powerful than God's moons. And by that same token or rather blasphemous belief, the white men were superior to God.

'*Kwakuti mwana wamisisi tingamukunde hondo iye akagona kutora mwedzi muchena ndokuiisa muchitima kuti uvhenekere mabhoyi nevarungu. Hodaaa seka zvako mwana waRaisoni naVhairedhi. Hakuna zvakadaro ndopika nambuya vangu Ruwiza vari pachuru ini.*'

That statement, laced with political connotations, attracted or rather drew a barrage mixture of murmurs of disapproval as well as bursts of laughter from fellow passengers. Some could be heard roundly condemning Amaiguru Roffinna for her shallow mindedness that exuded a shocking inferiority complex.

Others who were nationalistic in nature pitied her and sighed, '*Asingazive ngaadzidziswe.*' To be blunt, most of the questions asked by Amaiguru Roffinna were stupid and exposed her poor and remote background. Most of those questions would leave fellow passengers in stitches with laughter.

She had once asked, '*Nhai Rotario, sei miti yekuno ichiita nhangemutange nechitima asi yekwedu isingagoni kudhanaira zvako?'*

In a desperate bid to save face, Bhudhi Rotario would pretend to be snoring away, but Amaiguru Roffinna would have none of that. She would shake him violently so that he would keep her company.

But then keeping her company and motor mouthed as she was, was tantamount to making him a joint laughing stock.

Bhudhi Rotario could unknowingly have been paying through the nose for disregarding the gods' advice. He heaved a huge sigh of relief when Amaiguru Roffinna drifted into dreamland. By then, the majority of fellow passengers in their coach had also retired to snoreland.

Amaiguru Roffinna who had finally slept like a baby following a welcome ceasefire from the diarrhoea siege that had besieged her the previous night, had to be awaken by Bhudhi Rotario so that she could prepare for their disembarkment and the journey that lay ahead. After alighting from the train at the Umtali Railway Station, Bhudhi Rotario and Amaiguru Roffinna shoved their belongings into a Scooter tricycle taxi that wheeled them off to Mudzviti Bus Terminus. Scooters were cheaper than Renault 4 taxis. Mudzviti was an administration centre that catered for Africans who were barred from visiting the central business centre.

They were required to transact whatever business of theirs in downtown where business people of the Asian community, of Indian extraction would entice them with, *'Buya tinapangana'*.

At Mudzviti Bus Terminus, the pair intended to board a Zimunya bound bus that would drop them at the next bus stop that was just after the Fern Valley turn off.

Amaiguru Roffinna was perplexed by the skyscraper that towered over Mudzviti bus terminus. Apart from being mesmerized by the imposing architectural attraction, she also feared it would collapse and bury them under her debris. As a result, she kept on tugging at Bhudhi Rotario's immaculate safari suit leaving it crispy and badly soiled.

That drama by Amaiguru Roffinna left Bhudhi Rotario with a big rotten egg yoking down his handsome face in rivulets. He regretted his decision of having defied the gods.

As sweat of shame trickled down his body, he counted off the costs of marrying a total stranger. He abhorred the courtship method that he had settled for.

A method whose results had courted the ire of Tete Rhubhineti and the gods. A method whose results were likely to be disputed and disapproved by Mudhara and Amai. Bhudhi Rotario and Amaiguru Roffinna finally ambled into the Zimunya bound bus when it finally wormed its way into the terminus.

He found an empty seat for two, which he occupied with Amaiguru Roffinna. She chose to sit next to the window for she was fond of resting her arm on the bus window.

The other reason why she had settled next to the window was the fact that she still had a lot to see. She was still learning the ropes and etiquettes of travelling by public transport. The only public transport she had grown up riding was Baas Rustenburg's farm tractor.

CHAPTER 10

THE SCENE

Amaiguru Roffinna created yet another scene when the bus appeared swallowed, regurgitated and spewed by the flyover bridge. She yelled out a wail that sliced through the peace and tranquillity that had been reigning on the bus.

'Ko zvandave kumedzwa neninga yeGonawapotera zve nhai midzimu yangu, ndanyanyotadzei nhai vari kumafura mhepo?'

Gonawapotera was a cave that was found in a blood curdling Shona novel that was being broadcast over the radio under the Literature Bureau programme in the 70s. We would not want to miss any of that programme.

The presenters would make the reading as vivid and lively as they come. The presenters would always leave us in suspense with the words, *'Kuti varwi vaMambo vakazokwanisa kubata svori iya ngatichiregai kuita zvekufungidzira ngatiteererei zvakaitika muchikamu chinotevera panguva dzakafanana nedzino mangwana.'*

The following evening, we would huddle around our portable wooden curved radio trying to follow up on the unfolding drama. Those were the days when every evening most nationalistic minded blacks would converge around small radios to listen to The Voice of Maputo.

'Pamberi nehondo, pamberi mberi nehondo, alluta continua, abasha Ian Smith, *abasha mapuruvheya,'*

The voices of Cde Webster Shamu norm de guere Cde Charles Ndhlovu and company would thunder through. We would listen to songs like *Kune Nzira Dzemasoja.*

That programme would leave our hearts burning with a desire to join the Chimurenga War, even though we would have just graduated from our nappies. Such was the dynamite power of the programme.

The programme would leave us seething with anger over atrocities that were being committed by whites over our people whose land and cattle they had stolen, parcelled out and plundered at will. The programme would revitalise, reinvigorate, rejuvenate, uplifted our waning energies and spirits that would have been bombarded by the then Smith regime's propaganda machine.

In most towns and cities, the Smith regime having realised the importance of information dissemination and the poverty that reeked through black communities, had installed some loudspeakers at most public places through which they would broadcast their propaganda.

Most black men would stream out through thoroughfares or sanitary lanes, *masendiraini* to listen to such propaganda, which those nationalistic by nature or design would then compare and contrast with news they would have been fed by The Voice of Maputo.

Once the propaganda laced news was over, black men, most of them clad in shorts would stream back into their homes where poverty gladly awaited them with inviting arms.

After travelling for close to half an hour, Bhudhi Rotario and Amaiguru Roffinna alighted from the Zimunya bound bus. They struggled with their luggage that took its toll on their pace.

A few yards from the homestead away in Fern Valley, Bhudhi Rotario left behind Amaiguru Roffinna hiding behind a thick bush and strode through the home stretch alone. After what seemed like eternity, Bhudhi Rotario emerged from home with a hired aunt to take Amaiguru Roffinna through her paces.

Tradition or custom then demanded that a new daughter-in-law was not supposed to gate crush into the homestead of her in-laws unannounced.

Protocol then demanded that she had to be accompanied by her aunt who would keep her face covered with a veil like those worn by Moslem women. The aunt would be tagging her along for a few steps, stopped and only resumed when some money would have been thrown on the path that lead to the homestead.

CHAPTER 11

THE UNVEILING CEREMONY

The aunt would pick it up and move a few steps with her niece in tow before stopping dead in her tracks to pick up money that would have been thrown around by family members and close family friends. That custom was known as *kushonongora*, setting free.

The process would be repeated until the aunt and her niece entered the homestead amid pomp and fanfare.

Songs that sought to glorify the man for having done a world of good or a huge favour by marrying a star-crossed lady would be sung laced with zeal, zest, verve and gusto.

'*Hona Roffinna dai pasina Bhudhi vedu Roti waizoroorwa negudo resango. Chokwadi here dai pasina Bhudhi vedu Roti waizoroorwa negudo resango...*' the songs would be repeated with wild intemperance and monotony for a good measure just to spite rivals.

A lump sum of dollars would be demanded by the aunt to unveil the bride, *mwenga*. Once that money was paid, the aunt would get to unveil the bride. The unveiling would draw a lot of giggles, sneers, jeers and cynical comments from the in-laws' family, all aimed to unsettle as well as test the bride's temper and character. Once she passed the litmus test, she would be welcomed into the family at least for that night. The following morning, the daughter-in-law and her aunt would be required to be the earliest birds. They would sweep the yard, leaving some mounds of rubbish in the yard uncollected. They would also warm water to enable every family member to wash their faces. The daughter in-law would smear every family member with some cooking oil from her *chinu* container, which she would have brought to her in-laws as part of her dowry.

Only the father and mother-in-laws would be spared this chinu oil smearing business. Chinu and mombe yechimanda, a sacred cow, represented virginity or purity.

The rubbish would only get to be collected once money was placed on each and every heap. The daughter-in-law would accord due respect to every member of her new family.

That respect would also be extended to pets like dogs and cats. Even birds both domestic and those from the air would also be treated with shocking respect. However, after a few months, especially after the daughter-in-law would have fallen pregnant, she would descend on the pets and birds with chilling ruthlessness kicking and punching with venom never seen before.

This was the process that Amaiguru Roffinna had to go through at our homestead even though she had not brought along an aunt of her own.

That process was usually done by those who would not have eloped, but by those who would have followed proper marriage rites known as *kuperekwa*, those who would have been accompanied to their in-laws after payment of the bride price.

Three months down the line, after all the pomp and fanfare that accompanied her arrival, she started to show her true colours. She would become moody whenever she was supposed to cook family meals.

She would retire early to her bedroom feigning a migraine headache. Rumour had it that she was tight fisted. Once she retired to bed, she would be munching her favourite Choice Assorted biscuits, which she would drown with Mazoe Orange.

She would not even dole some of the biscuits to our two nieces and me. We were the youngest at the homestead and still had a few years before we could enrol for our primary education.

A child would only be able to attend school once they were able to touch their left ear with their right hand. The test was for the right hand to roll over their head before touching their left ear.

Others were required to lose all the milk teeth before being enrolled for primary education. Those privileged to have literate parents would enrol their children once they attained the age of seven. That was then and this is now. Bhudhi Rotario would also withdraw from the court where Mudhara used to share with us words of wisdom as well as the family tree and history. It was there at the court where we would listen to The Voice of Maputo and other radio programmes.

Not once, not twice, not thrice, but a number of times I had eavesdropped into Bhudhi Rotario and Amaiguru Roffinna's bedroom.

I had heard Amaiguru Roffinna who would have complained of a nagging splitting headache earlier on, bursting under bursts of laughter.

Once food was brought into her room, she would pretend to be under excruciating pain, groaning and moaning with pain. She would only talk by way of signs. But once whoever would have served her with food, took their leave, she would be back to her jovial mood.

Under one of my spying missions, I had heard her persuading Bhudhi Rotario to move in with his employers in Fern Valley. When Bhudhi Rotario would not yield, she became moodier and withdrew to herself.

She would refuse to participate in any household chores. She accused my sisters as well as Amai of having ganged up against her. She accused my sisters and Amai of gossiping about her every time she was absent.

As the cold war between Amaiguru Roffinna, Amai and our sisters raged on, Amaiguru was struck off the cooking duty rooster. Rumour had it that she was not good at cooking. Apart from not being a skilled cook, she was also accused of being unhygienic.

Rumour had it that she would blow off her nose, wipe the mucus with the back of her hand, smear the mucus on the hearth, before smearing the remainder on her legs which always gave them a shiny and glassy appeal.

After which, she would not wash her hands, but would continue to prepare meals as if nothing would have happened. That was the rumour that got her struck off the kitchen duty roaster.

When Amaiguru Roffinna got wind off the duty roaster debacle and what she termed as a conspiracy, she wept bitterly and locked herself in her bedroom. She later embarked on a food strike and threatened to pack her bags for Mazoe. The rumour had played well into her plan. She hoped to use that rumour to force Bhudhi Rotario to move over to Fern Valley.

The family knew that she would not starve off to death as she had an array of foodstuffs stashed away in her bedroom. When Bhudhi Rotario heard the rumour, he flew into a rage and threatened to beat up our sisters whom he accused of brewing, simmering, fermenting and frothing the rumour that had spread like a veld fire.

He tenaciously fought in his wife's corner threatening to move house to Fern Valley where he intended to stay in a vacant servant's or boys' quarters.

As head of the family, Mudhara desperately tried to bring the warring parties together for a peaceful resolution, but none of the factions were prepared for a truce. None of the warring parties were prepared to smoke the peace pipe.

Disappointed by the new twist of events and Amai's unpalatable history of shenanigans, Mudhara moved over to Fern Valley. A few days later, with no peaceful settlement to the haggling, Bhudhi Rotario and Amaiguru Roffinna also relocated to Fern Valley.

Everyone blamed Amaiguru Roffinna for having driven a wedge between Amai and Mudhara. She was accused of having masterminded the breaking down of the family unity that used to exist before she assumed the family name.

Amai would sing, *'Waparadza musha wangu ndiRoffinnia, haiwa iwa waparadza musha waparadza musha wangu ndiRoffinnia haiwa iwa waparadza musha,'*

But Amaiguru Roffinna believed she was under siege from Amai and our sisters who wanted to push her out of the family she had married into without the blessings of the gods. Amai believed that Bhudhi Rotario's marriage to Amaiguru Roffinna was cursed the moment the gods disapproved it.

As the war intensified, the Williams under whose employment Mudhara and Bhudhi Rotario were, moved to Morningside, a leafy suburb in the Eastern side of Umtali. Mudhara and Bhudhi Rotario never bothered to check on us.

As the liberation war intensified, Amai secured a sanctuary in Dangamvura's A Section where she had my sisters Porina and Tambudzai together with Bhudhi Maikoro holed up.

Chapter 12

Running Scared

Amai and I remained at home, which then resembled a phantom haunted homestead. It was deserted, no longer homely, appeared scruffy and was desperately weeping for a routine facelift. The homestead suffered abject neglect.

Amai would prepare our supper early in the evening to enable us to retire to bed early. Sometimes we would go and sleep over at one of our neighbours, the Kupakwedengas.

Luckily, for Amai, she never ran short of company as she quickly swayed the heart of a guerrilla detachment commander Cde Tichakunda Mabhunu.

Times without number, the commander would come and sleep over with Amai on her matrimonial bed. I no longer understood the relationship that existed between Amai and Mudhara.

Maybe I was naïve to realise that Mudhara and Amai were on separation. What I enjoyed most about the *separation* was the fact that it heralded peace and tranquillity in the home.

Fights and verbal contests that had become part of the family setup had vanished. Tantrums, obscene words that used to be thrown around or hurled over thick and fast, had ceased to fly by. Indeed, a ceasefire was being observed albeit not officially.

I was burning inside. I could not pluck up enough courage to confront Amai on her newly found lover. I had to be chucked out of her matrimonial bedroom to accommodate the comrade. I could not challenge Cde Tichakunda Mabhunu.

He was an imposing figure who was muscular and always armed to the teeth. I once thought of striking him dead in his sleep with a machete, but I just could not pluck enough courage needed to execute my plan. Legend had it that he had been cooked with muti that made him immortal. Enemy bullets that once tried to pierce through his body had turned into water. He was a Terminator incarnate, so I was once made to believe.

He would not die once, but nine times just like the proverbial cat. If he were to die finally, he would reappear or resurrect in another country. I had no one to share my pain with. I had no sibling to fight over blankets with. I had no sibling to wrestle over a juice chunk of meat with.

I had no sibling to hackle over trivialities with. I was a lone ranger. I terribly missed everyone. I desperately needed companionship. I longed for company.

I had no one to engage in hide and seek with. The court where we used to pass time during the evenings was no longer welcoming. I would not dare visit the court where I would sit in seclusion.

There was nothing to suggest that this was the place where we used to sit it out listening to Mudhara's rumbling, winding and sometimes boring lifetime social lectures.

There we had listened to various radio programmes among them the inspirational *Voice of Maputo* on which the slogan, *'Pamberi mberi nehondo!'* would boom over and through.

There we had enjoyed and shared some family lighter moments. There we had listened to music of our time. There we had danced to the traditional beat of *Katekwe*, serenaded to contemporary music that were both inspirational both lyrically and instrumentally.

There I had listened and witnessed my brothers going through their paces musically. There I had witnessed Bhudhi Rotario strumming his favourite tunes of love with flowing expertise.

There I had witnessed the other two brothers of mine Maikoro and Mairosi strumming some homemade guitars *wandiramba x 3 ... kurambana hakuna mhosva, nyora tsamba x 3...*

There we had crafted wire cars and some small wooden wheel carts, *ngoro* on which we would ride. We sometimes shaped the wheels from some logs using a traditional carving tool, *mbezo*.

Rubberised wheels from defunct lawn mowers or perambulators made better wheel carts. Poor and always short of toys, I would chisel out some common bricks into makeshift toy buses, which I would push around the yard.

I would miss the good old times when I used to go to Dora River to bath and fish. A few years before the war of Chimurenga intensified, the river was rich in protein as it brimmed over with breams and other species. Fresh waters then cascaded and meandered gracefully and promenading with the gait of a peacock.

The banks were then lined with scrumptious, luscious or succulent grass that shone brightly under the sunlight gaze. Women would flock or troop to the river for some laundry, which they would spread to dry on the stretch of smooth rocks known in Shona as *ruware*.

On the smooth rocks, we would slide it out whilst sitting on some slippery tree branches of species known as *nhanzva*. That slithering game was known as *mutserendende*. It caused havoc on our shorts leaving most of them weeping for patches thereby perpetuating the nickname *MaTV*.

Synonymous with other rivers in communities elsewhere, women gossipers then would converge at the river for the latest and juiciest piece of news from the community. The rumour mill will spin, tumble, wheel and turn into overdrive.

Naturally, some Peeping Toms who should have been arraigned before the conventional courts to answer charges of *Crimen Injuria*, would then synonymously, clandestinely and stealthily tiptoed to the river to catch glimpses of naked women bathing and gambolling in the water.

The Romeos and Juliets of the community would stampede, jostle, stumble, fall on each other and grovel to meet at the river, which they had turned into a rendezvous and love nest.

The river would sing melodiously in enticing crescendos for us like what Tyrose Tendaupenyu of the *Furuwa* fame used to do for us.

Then the river would flow her heart out and croon like what Jamal Mataure and the diminutive songbird Betty Makaya did on the *Kurwizi* duet. The river resembled great Safirio *Mukadota* Madzikatire's *KwaHunyani*.

The Romeos and Juliets of that time would frolic, regale, wriggle, wiggle and gyrate seductively under the beat of the flowing river. That was then.

The river then resembled a myriad of a grotesque abyss or chasm of a grey mass of granite boulders whose tongues stuck out in readiness for a French kiss that came in the form of a deluge.

To us something phenomenal, mystic and supernatural was taking place. Nature had over those years turned her deaf ears to our distress calls. It had closed her eyes and seemed to have drifted into a big deep slumber of the Creator.

Not even a violent wake-up call would have awakened her up from dreamland for she too had reminisced those old jolly good old days when she looked vivacious, exuberant, energetic and gorgeous. Her skin then was velvet, radiant, smooth and soft to the touch as a parrot's breast. It was dazzling to the eye under the glare of the sun, an undisputed community belle, the environment, the river. That reminded me of Michael Lanas' scorcher *The River.*

It appeared the river had also joined the Chimurenga War in protest against white occupation. The river seemed to have been waging her own war of liberation against white land occupiers.

Even the gods of the land had risen against white rule. The bones of Mbuya Nehanda had risen as she had boldly declared and prophesied before she was sentenced to death by hanging. The Chimurenga War was raging and razing through the country.

So deep was the Chimurenga euphoria, that it could be touched. The rapture of Chimurenga war that was sweeping the countryside appeared to be tangible and contagious. Death was no longer feared but embraced. Death then appeared to have befriended us.

We would sing, *'Amai nababa ndati musandicheme kana ndafa nehondo.'*

We were all drugged with the spirit of Chimurenga War. During the day, Amai and I would swim with the tide of Chimurenga War, but when night fell, we would cringe whenever our dogs barked importunately. I gaudily recall one melancholy night when a group that consisted of seven heavily armed chivalrous guerrillas under the command of Cde Tichakunda Mabhunu marched into our homestead.

Our dogs barked before whimpering and scurrying away for cover after catching the smell of bullets from bandoliers that dangled on the shoulders of the freedom fighters. We were made to believe that, the strong smell of gunpowder and bullets could scare away witches, wizards and spectres. I had never come across freedom fighters. They wore fatigues that were complimented with some tree branches that draggled treacherously from the ribbons of their hats. Two of the freedom fighters strode onto the yard, leaving the other five in strategic positions and ready for an assault should a gun fire exchange ensue.

Those who had taken cover only relaxed after being issued with an all clear sign by Cde Mabhunu. Whenever Cde Mabhunu stamped his booted foot on the floor, an armed subordinate of his would enter the kitchen. Thus, legend then had it that freedom fighters used to live in military boots.

Amai had to quickly rekindle a dying fire, prepare sadza with two chickens and fried eggs as accompanying relish. Freedom fighters then would not touch okra hence the song, *'Gandanga Haridye Derere Mukoma Rinozorwara.'*

It was not only taboo for freedom fighters not to eat sadza with okra, but even those with boxing or fighting muti, *mangoromera* were barred from eating okra as it would weaken their fighting prowess.

I was charmed by Cde Mabhunu's philosophies. A University of Rhodesia Political Science student dropout and a Peking-Beijing trained guerrilla, he appeared to have eaten from the same plate with Cde Mao Zedong.

He followed Cde Zedong's military thinking to the dot. Cde Zedong likened the masses to water and freedom fighters to fish, which would not survive without water, and therefore the two had to co-exist with each other.

Young as I was, I was charmed by Cde Mabhunu's public relations. After the freedom fighters had had their fill, they left behind two cases of tinned beef to replace the two chickens they had hungrily wolfed.

They advised Amai to dispose the empty beef tins into a lavatory. They also opined to Amai to sweep away their footprints as they could land us into trouble with the Rhodesian Forces.

CHAPTER 13

THE TORTURE

Two days later, some Selous Scouts who were fighting alongside the Rhodesian Front picked up Amai and me. They suspected us of hosting freedom fighters. We were tortured and left for dead by the Rhodesian Special Branch.

We were forced to feast on our excreta as well as cattle dung in the process. Later Amai and I were ordered to join a group of villagers from Mambondiani in Dora who were facing similar charges.

We were all ordered to strip naked before being made to sit on some bare rocks that were under cordon from a sweltering October sun. We were ordered to face each other naked under that scorching sun.

No shame came over us as we were forced to partake in dehumanising antics by the soldiers who were enjoying the act under the shade of trees as they puffed away cigarette smoke into the atmosphere that was pregnant with tears of torture.

The soldiers intended to use us, as human shields should freedom fighters decided to attack them. We got released following the arrival of their trucks. The soldiers made sure that they would not just let us go without further humiliation. They picked on a middle-aged woman Amai Hedhiwigi who they ordered to be intimate with Sorobheti a lanky built twenty-year-old orphan who was twice her junior. The pair were forced to engage in bedroom scenes, which left them badly impaired.

The experienced Amai Hedhiwigi was forced to exhibit her bedroom antics in the presence of all and sundry.

At the end of the torturing session, all her bedroom antics had left a mark in the public domain. None of us found the acts amusing. It was war, it was an order we had to oblige with. It was an ordeal we had to undergo through.

We were obliged to do whatever the soldiers would have ordered us to do. They were a law unto themselves. Nobody could call them to order not even the court martial law. Court martial lawlessness reigned supreme. The law of the jungle existed and they were very much eager to perpetuate it. After all, they found joy in it. It oiled their cause.

Earlier on, we had witnessed two wretched war collaborators from Chatizemakumbo in Dora Pinto dying after being forced to devour three chameleons. Four other war collaborators had vicious dogs set upon them mauling them in the process before being dragged to their deaths by Puma military vehicles that were engaged in a drag race. They died gruesome deaths.

As if that was not enough, the quartet were repeatedly ran over by the heavy military vehicles that left them in a bloody pulp. That type of torture and mass killing was designed to instil fear into our hearts.

Instead of cowing us into submission, that action strengthened our resolve to free ourselves. We had suffered enough torture and desperately wanted our freedom, our independence, our uhuru our sovereignty, our identity, our country, our Zimbabwe.

The remainder of those who had been rounded up for interrogation vehemently denied the charge of harbouring freedom fighters. Instead, we promised to inform them as soon as we got wind of *magandanga's* presence in our area.

Two days later, the soldiers descended on our homestead in high spirits. To buy our loyalty and cooperation, Selous Scouts who were part of the group, dangled a succulent carrot before us, two cases of tinned beef and tubed margarine.

When the dust appeared to have settled, freedom fighters who had got wind of the presence of sell outs, *vatengesi* in the community, herded all and sundry to a central and vantage point within the community where they had set up a temporary base.

We were made to sing ourselves hoarse despite the fact that we were very close to Fern Valley, a white inhabited community. After psyching us with a litany of liberation war songs, Cde Muchademba Mabhunu broke into another song, 'Carpricorn Chenjera.' We all sang in unison with verve and gusto.

With those in attendance beginning to enjoy the serenading and drugging effect of the song, with tears cascading down his cheeks, Cde Muchademba Mabhunu broke into another song. Before we knew it, Cde Muchademba Mabhunu doubled over as if in a trance and fished out Mudhara Firimoni and his live-in girlfriend Amai Torpedo accusing them of being sell-outs. The pair was accused of having sold out freedom fighters to the Rhodesian Special Branch.

That tipoff had allegedly resulted in a skirmish with the Rhodesian Forces, near Kuhudzai village in Dora Pinto.

The shootout had resulted in the death of three freedom fighters and a dozen or so of the Rhodesian Forces who had died in action like what the Rhodesian propagandists always wanted the masses to believe. Mudhara Firimoni and Amai Torpedo were also accused of having volunteered information to the Rhodesian Special Branch on the movements of freedom fighters in our community.

This resulted in Amai and I being subjected to vigorous shock induced torturing that left us numb and nearly paralysed. The duo under a flood of tears, confessed to their sins.

They were later ordered to dig up their shallow graves in which they were going to be interred after judgment would have been delivered.

The sell-outs after being harangued, had their arms tied behind their backs, blindfolded, made to kneel in their shallow resting places before being ordered to say their last prayers to their ancestral spirits. Cde Muchademba Mabhunu having lectured us on the importance of having a unity of purpose, the reason why we all needed to prop up that war as well as the dangers of being informants to the white colonial establishment, ordered a lowly ranked combatant to hack the duo with a bayonet that protruded from his sub-machine gun.

The bayonet sliced through the necks of the two alleged sell-outs who slumped into the shallow graves Boko Haram and ISIS style. The children wailed and wept for the sins of their parents. Cde Mabhunu swiftly called the wailing children to order and admonished them for their actions. He warned them that such treatment could also be unleashed on them should they chose not to cooperate. After giving the siblings a hair dryer of a lecture, the two children were handed shovels with which to cover corpses of their parents.

'Kana mukaramba kufushira vatengesi ava tinokudimburai misoro futi nekuti mwana wenyoka inyoka nekudaro mwana wemutengesi mutengesi,' declared a seething Cde Mabhunu.

The two complied and covered their parents with mounds of soil amid song and kongonya dance from the freedom fighters and members of the community. Another sell-out Komukomu was also picked out and ordered to stand at the middle of a raging bon fire that surrounded him.

He sweated profusely from the debilitating effects of the heat from the bonfire. Before long, he had passed out before succumbing to the roasting effect of the oven hot heat wave. He died a painful death.

He died a gruesome death. He remained mummified for weeks on end. Cde Mabhunu had ordered us not to bury him, but to leave him at the mercy of wild dogs and hyenas.

In unison, our hearts palpitated with trepidation. In unison, we were drenched with sweat of consternation. In unison and in silence, we vowed never to betray the spirit of Chimurenga.

In unison, we made some stands, never to throw spanners into the wheels of the runaway freedom train.

We sang our hearts right into the dead of the night. We sang ourselves hoarse right into the ears of the white community.

We no longer feared death and instead death feared us. We were no longer running scared of whites, instead whites were then running scared of us for they believed we had been turned into zombies. We were not zombies but supporters of nationalists. We buttressed what our nationalist leaders stood for. We fought for freedom, dreamt freedom and shared dishes with freedom fighters.

We mixed and mingled with them as well as behaving like them. At the end of the day, we viewed ourselves as freedom fighters, we talked like freedom fighters and their bravery had rubbed onto us.

We behaved like cats. We behaved like immortals. The raging spirit of Chimurenga had consumed us.

I vividly recall the day when Nhamodzenyika and I were sent out on a reconnaissance mission into the city of Umtali before planting a parcel bomb in an empty state owned United Passenger Company bus. The bomb later detonated blowing the heavy machine into pieces. When we heard news of the sabotage over the radio, we glowed with satisfaction and pride.

Three days later, Amai and I joined Bhudhi Maikoro and sisters Porina and Tambudzai in Dangamvura where we sought bolthole after we got wind of the news that the Rhodesian Special Services Branch that had had received information about my part on the blowing up of the bus, were closing in for the kill.

Somebody must have blown away my cover. I was wanted dead or alive. A young terrorist I was called. A young saboteur I was labelled. A young renegade, my image was soiled.

A young and lethal insurgency, I was portrayed as one. I was none of those. I was a young freedom fighter, a toy soldier of freedom.

CHAPTER 14

FLAMES OF POVERTY

That small room in Dangamvura accommodated Amai, Bhudhi Maikoro, Tambudzai, Porina and I. The trio were attending the local Sheni Primary School.

Bhudhi Maikoro who was a no nonsense brother, a strict disciplinarian, would always whip us in line whenever he felt we were going out of step with family dictates. He slept with the landlord's sons who were his age mates. Our family was under siege from poverty.

Amai had to join fellow poor women from Dangamvura in establishing some green grocers' stalls. She would join other women from the hood who would go and buy some vegetables from Weir Mouth for resale in Dangamvura.

The family would resort to using vegetables and tomatoes that would have gone bad for relish. It was logical not to use fresh vegetables and tomatoes for relish as that would have eaten into the profits.

Sometimes I would accompany Amai to Sakubva River where we would scavenge for *konorosi*, a type of relish that was popular with poor ghetto families. Konorosi grew along the banks of Sakubva River.

My brother and I together with our landlord's sons, would queue near Dangamvura Beer Hall, Chigomba to hustle and bustle for some delicacies.

We would get to see some drunkards staggering home under the influence of Kariba Mhamba. We would get to see some drunkards engaging in foul-mouthed contests. We would get to see some drunkards wheeling home with some ladies of the night who they would have baited with some mugfuls of Kariba Mhamba. Fights would occasionally break out among us as we fought for some selling points.

We had to be tough to survive. I vividly recall one cold night when the sound of gunfire thundered, rattled and ricocheted into the neighbourhood from mountains.

A driver of a bus that belonged to the State who was returning to the city to knock off, was caught off just near Dangamvura Filling station.

The bus was hit by a mortar whose impact saw it swerving and landing into a ditch facing Sakubva River. We were later told that the driver died on the spot.

The following morning, some youths from the ghetto could be seen helping themselves to some coins from the bus wreckage. The boys intended to use the money to pay for their entrance at Dangamvura Beit Hall where bioscopes where shown.

Dangamvura became a target by freedom fighters after the Smith Regime foolishly allocated some houses to some soldiers in the P Section. Freedom fighters did not trust black urban dwellers who they believed were turncoats, traitors or *vatengesi*. Freedom fighters then believed that black urban dwellers were oiling the settlers' machinery. Some black urbanites who had been sent to school by some missionaries ended up thinking like white settlers, freedom fighters reasoned.

They would have been brainwashed into thinking that the Second Chimurenga War was a senseless war. A war that was being waged by some senseless blacks who were barbaric, savages, archaic and illiterate.

Blacks who were simply bent on reversing the gains of the three Cs touted as having been brought to Africa by whites. The three Cs stood for Commerce, Civilization and Christianity.

Following that attack on the State bus, which the regime pronounced as sabotage, the Rhodesian soldiers mounted their wheeled rocket launchers at the then luscious Dangamvura Golf Course facing the Manicaland Provincial Heroes Acre.

The Golf Course has since been occupied by part of Dangamvura's Area 3 Section. Now that mounting of artillery by the Rhodesian soldiers at the periphery of the suburb facing the other periphery where freedom fighters had once laid siege from, was dangerous.

Should the war have broken out, residents were going to be caught up in a crossfire. By then, we had moved to the P Section of the same hood near Dangamvura High School. The RF soldiers had advised residents to slip under their beds whenever they heard sounds of gunfire. Luck to those who had beds under which they would take refugee.

We did not have any bed and that would mean, should the warring parties resolve to exchange fire, which was highly likely, we would perish under some debris.

The following morning, whilst listening to Chamunorwa, a song of the moment then by Tinei Chikupo, I was taken aback by the stance that had been taken by the Rhodesian soldiers who had mounted their heavy artillery at the golf course.

Another song, a choral one that was solemnly sung by Rujeko Primary School choir, moved the entire staff and pupils that day.

The choir's conductor a Mr Chitakatira painted a teary figure as he led his choir in the song, *'Nhamo imbiri woye, nhamo imbiri vakomana, nhamo imbiri woye nhamo imbiri vasikana ndendende, ndendende.'* The song touched on trials, tribulations and troubles. The neighbourhood was under siege.

CHAPTER 15

DAWN OF A NEW ERA

Soon after ceasefire, we joined youths, women and men from the ghetto in campaigning. We would toyi toyi around the suburb singing some revolutionary songs.

We would toyi toyi around the suburb singing revolutionary songs like Maruza Vapambepfumi. A new euphoria had just swept across the country. A new wave of euphoria had just dazzled the new nation.

At the helm of the new nation was the world's most educated leader Cde Robert Gabriel Mugabe who then had seven degrees to his name, two of them Masters. He had studied Law, Economics and a Bachelor of Arts among others.

We were all charmed by his speech at the Zimbabwe Grounds. We were all held spellbound by his maiden speech at Rufaro Stadium that marked the country's independence from the white settlers. We all envied the Prime Minister Cde Mugabe.

We all strived to emulate him academically. We all strived to ape his orator ship skills. He became the darling of Western countries after he had successfully extended the hand of reconciliation to white Rhodesians including former Prime Minister Ian Douglas Smith. The international community led by Britain and the United States of America conferred Cde Mugabe with honorary degrees and a Knighthood. He had walked the talk of reconciliation.

He had urged the nation to turn guns into ploughshares. He had called upon all and sundry to smoke the peace pipe. He went about reconstructing the battered nation.

Five year economic and social services road maps or blue prints like, Gore Remasimba Evanhu, Gore Rekushandura Zvinhu, Gore Regutsa Ruzhinji, Houses for All, Health for All, Vision 2020, were rolled out. Education was made free.

As a result, a good number of refugees and freedom fighters who had seen action during the liberation struggle, but had been demobilised after failing to make the grade into the conventional Zimbabwe National Army, enrolled at Dangamvura High School.

That was how the school then came to be known in the

neighbourhood as Dzapasi. We were told Dzapasi was one of the assembly points that housed freedom fighters after ceasefire came into effect.

We were also told in muted tones, that the bulk of those guys would refuse to undergo corporal punishment and would threaten to beat the hell out of teachers, some of whom were younger than them.

When Zimbabwe attained independence, we moved to Tendai Hostels in the heart of the light industrial area near Yeovil medium density suburb. The flat was a drop-in centre for refugees and war collaborators who did not have a place they could call home.

We stayed there for a month before we were moved to Sakubva's McGreggors Section near the Avenues.

We stayed there for three days before my family was moved by the Social Welfare Department to a Road Department compound just outside Fern Valley and just before Blue Desert Store.

I remained behind in Sakubva with a single distant relative of Amai, Amainini Rusiya. I had once stayed with Amainini Rusiya in the late 70s. During both stints in Sakubva, I had picked up some traits that would leave me wallowing in murky waters of trouble.

Still, there was no sight of Mudhara, Bhudhi Rotario and Amaiguru Roffinna. Even Sisi Gaudenziya, her husband Mukuwasha Furikwenzi and Bhudhi Mairosi seemed to have turned their backs on us. Amai struggled to fend for us. Mudhara had walked out on us.

He could not bother to check on us. To him, we no longer existed. We were being punished for sins that we had not committed. We were being punished for Amai's tomfooleries. We were under siege from a social and economic war in which we had no say. We were viewed as pawns in a game of chess. Decoys that was what we were. Mudhara was trying to get back at Amai using us as pawns in a game of chess in which he had assumed the grandmaster title.

It was time for Amai to be submissive. Mudhara then held the keys to the family's livelihood. The game had suddenly changed. The once hunted bird had surprisingly wrestled the catapult from the hunter.

One day, Amai decided to visit Mudhara in the Morningside area where he was holed up. Upon arrival, she was greeted with a single lady a nannie at the Williams. The lady Mavis whose name had been corrupted to Movhesi had moved in with Mudhara.

Amai gave Movhesi a beating of her lifetime. When Mudhara

realised that her newly found love had been pummelled, he tried to restrain Amai, but he too got some thumping. To save face, he had to call the Williams who threatened to call the police.

When the storm calmed down, the Williams ordered Mudhara to take good care of his family or else he would be relieved off his duties. He promised to turn over a new leaf. Mudhara also promised to sever his ties with Movhesi.

During all that hullaballoo, Bhudhi Rotario and Amaiguru Roffinna who then was suckling her first child Ndaiziveyi, watched the drama from a distance. The duo did not want to get involved in the unfolding drama. Amaiguru Roffinna had not taken lightly to how Amai and my sisters had allegedly connived to have her jettisoned out of the family compound on scandalous charges. She had vowed never to forgive Amai and my sisters for what she had perceived to be a diabolical act.

Bhudhi Rotario and Amaiguru Roffinna seemed to have turned their backs on Amai and us. When Amai showed up at their door intending to see Ndaiziveyi her grandchild, the duo could not let her in.

Instead of letting her into the room, Bhudhi Rotario had to show Ndaiziveyi to Amai by hoisting her through a window. Amai had to see her grandchild through the window.

With tears trickling down her cheeks, Amai threw down her wrapping shawl, *shawero*, an act that could result in a parental curse. A curse that could result in a truckload of misfortunes.

She swiftly picked the shawero up and vowed never to visit Bhudhi Rotario and Amaiguru Roffinna again. Not in her lifetime, she had asserted.

They just could not allow her to hold and cuddle her grandchild. She had wronged them big time and to them she was no longer their child's grandmother. Their child deserved a better granny. On the other hand, we also felt they had gone too far.

Amai deserved a better treatment not the bunkum treatment they had subjected her to. With all due respect, we all believed that despite what had transpired, Amai would remain Amai and nobody could take her place. She was irreplaceable and needed to be honoured.

After the incident, Mudhara would visit us asking about problems that we faced. He appeared and acted alien to us. Surely how could he ask us about problems that we had been facing after having disappeared from the family radar for nearly a decade?

He must have been drugged with shame and was struggling to fit into our system of life. I was enrolled for my Grade 1 at Sheni Primary School in Dangamvura after having celebrated my thirteenth birthday.

We would walk and run to school barefooted for almost 20 kilometres to and from. Sometimes we would board buses from Sheni to Mutare Teachers' College for 5cents. I remember one day how we were caught unawares by a cent increment on bus fares.

We were short of 3c that is my two nieces and I. A Good Samaritan in the form of a nurse saved us from the blushes of the bus conductor who had threatened to throw us from of the bus that was coughing, spitting, spluttering and splitting her way towards the city via Munezhu.

We dropped off at Mutare Teachers' College and walked the remainder of the journey home barefooted. That we always did. We would visit the school toilet barefooted oblivious of health hazards like bilharzia. Almost a quarter of fellow students would come to school barefooted. There were some poor families from Dangamvura and the environs of Dora Dombo like Vhirindi, Magodhlo, Chatizamakumba and Mhandambiri who would also trudge to school barefooted.

Our parents under cordon from poverty could not afford to buy us even the cheapest pairs of plastic shoes, Sandaks for both boys and girls.

CHAPTER 16

THE WINDING QUEUE

In winter those from Dora Dombo would rumble to school, clutching some hot stones wrapped with papers to fend off cold. At Sheni, Grades Ones to Three would queue for milk during break time.

All we were required to bring to school were plastic cups, or some plastic yeast tumblers in which milk would be poured into. We would accompany that milk with fat cakes.

Every morning, all primary schools would receive their allocation of jerry cans filled with milk for distribution among infants or kindergartens. We really enjoyed our breaks then.

Those from upper grades who would have been weaned off from the lactating mother, the jerry cans, would poke fun at us *accusing* us of drinking donkey milk. We were not bothered at all. We knew that those were statements from a disgruntled lot.

After break, we would troop, shuffle and patter into our classrooms for radio lessons. We would take some instructions from an alien teacher who would be broadcasting over the radio. Our teachers would assist us with some instructions that we would have failed to comprehend. We would listen to some songs like, *'Granny in the kitchen doing a little stitching, then comes the ghost and pushes grannie out,',* *'Dance around together in the sunny weather till we, till we all fall down,'.* We would also sing, *'Old McDonald had a farm, iya...iya woo!'*

We would read some children's novels like Puss In Boots, without a shade of shame. But nowadays puss means something else.

We would sing joyously in our oversized uniforms, 'Are you happy, are you gay?' Then that was not an offensive statement, but today most people will take offence if asked that question.

We lived in a world of bewilderment, a world of wonders, a world that we could not understand, a world of mystery. Our teachers then enjoyed keeping us in that numinous world of ours.

That kept radio lessons shrouded in secrecy and mystery. That kept us glued to those super lessons dished out by super teachers.

We would always try so hard to respect those female teachers from another space. Sometimes those mysterious teachers, our mistresses as female teachers were referred to as, would lead us in reading lessons.

We read such books like Mapatya, Karume Kanoruta, Mushamba Richakwata, Datya Gadzi, Zidyavanhu Mugomo, Kukurukura Hunge Wapotswa, China Manenji Hachifambisi, Kutonhodzwa KwaChauruka, Karikoga Gumi Remiseve, Kusasana Kunoparira, Akafuratidzwa Moyoand Sungai Mbabvu. Other stories that we read were Mupugunyoni The Night Ape, Bongwi the Baboon, Umsolopogasi, Sister Florence Nightingale, Luis Pasteur, The Adventures of Huckleberry Finn, The Voyages of Christopher Columbus, Vasco Da Gama's Exploits, David Livingstone's Discovery of the Victoria Falls, Chipo's Big Hat, Farai NaFarisai, Benny and Betty as well as Ndombo, The Hardy Boys, The Nancy Drew series, Enid Blyton but not Mills and Boon series.

We would thunder in unison, 'Ona Ndombo, Ndombo ari mubhara rababa vake.' All household properties belonged to the man of the house.

In Grade 1, we read *Gogoi*, a book that signalled our enrolment into the first grade. In Grade 2, we read *Pindai*, a book that accommodated us at our new school. In Grade 3, we were taken through our educational paces through *Garai*, a book that took us through the comfort of our institutions and a journey that we would have thus travelled like Ebenezer.

In Grade 4, *Tandarai* the book enabled us to feel and enjoy the comfort of our institution as we passed time with the educative book. Grade 5, *Nakirwai*, a cruise aboard the education bandwagon.

The Grade 6, book *Budirirai* emphasized on progress and development and in Grade 7, we read Bvunzwai which touched on examinations which we were to sit for at the end of that academic year to signal the end of our learning curve at the lower school. We were also supposed to memorise The Students Companion by Wilfred D Best from cover to cover.

CHAPTER 17

THE REFLECTION

As we drifted into adolescence, we became more adventurous due to hormonal changes. We would strategically place some splintered specks of mirrors under girls' desks in order to get a glimpse of their undergarments.

Sometimes we would be fortunate, as some unfortunate girls would not be sporting any under garments due to a grinding poverty.

The daring ones who would be dying to compare and contrast under garments worn by lady teachers and those attired by primary school girls, would plant mirrors under female teachers' tables.

Most popular female pants then were decorated with a blossoming flower usually a rose, white or red and violets, which are always blue.

If the female teacher caught one, the punishment would be too ghastly to contemplate. As hormonal changes continued to take their toll on us, breaking our voices in the process, we would be engaged in contact games like netball and traditional games like Chisveru and Sarura Wako.

Naughty as we were, we would pretend to have missed our target and go straight for girls developing breasts. We would love the touch and feeling of plump and pointed breasts, breasts that were yet to be bridled with brassieres, then known in the township lingo as *mabhodhi*.

I vividly recall how Purudhenzi, a sexually active sister of a friend of mine in her early 20s once allowed me to have a feel of her boobs which had developed much and were ready for lactation.

That young lady was about to sit for her Ordinary Level at Dangamvura High School whilst I was two years shy of sitting for my first public examinations, Grade 7 examinations.

Purudhenzi who had seen action during the Second Chimurenga, had made an undertaking to avail herself whenever I felt like fondling her boobs. She would invite me to their house whenever she was alone. Inside her bedroom, she would undress in my full view.

She would dance seductively before my bulging shorts. She would allow me to suckle her breasts, fondle her backside before directing my manhood into her womanhood.

She would allow me unlimited access to her body. She would teach me some bedroom antics she would have enjoyed with her married boyfriend. She would moan and groan in perpetual pleasure.

I would *quench* her sexual appetite. She would spoil and pamper me with some freebies from her demobilization allowances.

Our carry-ons came to light when we were busted by the lady's grandmother who for some time had placed us under surveillance. When the shameful act got to my parents, it had been doctored or rather watered down.

Little did I know that I was being sexually abused by a major who was ripe for marriage. I strongly believed that it was part of growing up.

I only got to watch my first television programme when I was doing Grade 5 after Bhudhi Mairosi took Bhudhi Maikoro and me to his work place in Darlington. His employers had gone on a month-long holiday in Kariba.

We enjoyed the comfort of the Stephens' lounge. We got to enjoy the comfort of a set of sofas for the first time in our lives.

We got to watch television programmes which we would savour even though the television set was a black and white brand, the type that was housed in a wooden four legged cabinet of some sort. We got to watch some ornamental fish that wriggled in a glass fish tank.

We got to see some refrigerators, some kitchen dressers which we used to call cupboards at home, some display cabinets, a gramophone better than the one that was owned by Mudhara Mujubheki. We would tune to Radio 2 for local content as well as Radio 3 for Hitspick, which was later rebranded Hitsville.

We listened to artistes like Banana Rama, Cool and The Gang, Lionel Richie, Atlantic Star, John Nash, Jimmy Cliff, Eddie Grant, Michael Jackson of the Jacksons fame, Jonah Moyo, Zexie Manatsa, Thomas Mapfumo, Oliver M'tukudzi and Marshall Munhumumwe to mention only a few. We got to eat our first spiced meals whose aroma would envelope, entice and engulf the entire house.

We enjoyed the beauty of electricity, which we had become used to watch from as far afield as Dangamvura.

That sojourn was an eye opener. It showed us how poor we were, how poverty had kept us under siege with no salvation in sight. That stint under the care of Bhudhi Mairosi inspired us to do well at school.

It strengthened our determination to wiggle our way out of poverty. Stung by the siege of poverty, Bhudhi Mairosi also resolved to join Alpha Study Group in Sakubva to improve his academic background.

That type of poverty, which is engraved in the DNA, needs a special type of deliverance by the likes of Prophets Magaya and Makandiwa to be exorcised. It would appear like a generational curse.

CHAPTER 18

THE CONFIRMATION

A few households in Dangamvura were decorated with television sets then. A 14-inch black and white television set, a set of scotched sofas, the high back type that rocked on spring, a refrigerator and electric stove, were status symbols.

People would say, *'Mumba mavo mune zvese.'* Television aerials that towered above council owned houses in Dangamvura, were a sure confirmation of a working television set.

Only a few civil servants among them teachers, nurses, police officers and soldiers could afford to buy or rent television sets from Nolan's TV Sales and Hire, Kunzwana Credit Store as well as Nyore Nyore Zimbabwe Furnishers.

Those who hailed from poor families had harrowing experiences to tell whenever they visited their neighbours' comfortable houses for television viewing especially during popular programmes like World Wrestling Federation (WWF), Sounds On Saturday, Mvengemvenge and Mhuri yaVaMukadota drama series. None of them were allowed to sit on the sofas.

They were made to watch television whilst sitting huddled on the carpet or worse, on the bare floor. They were only allowed in after some body checks. Only those who would have passed through the bathroom were allowed in.

Some were made to turn their pockets insideout, as occupants of the house would be looking for those who might leave sand.

Sand, which they would have brought, tucked in their pockets from several playgrounds where they would have been engaged in ball matches.

Others were made to watch television from outside through a curtain that would have been drawn aside.

A friend of mine once confided in me how one day his friend's sister who no longer wanted him to watch their television, poured him a potful of watery left overs of sadza, *makoko.*

He went home shaking from hair to toe since it was a winter night. Children who hailed from fortunate families that owned television sets were held in high esteem and were simply untouchables. They could get away with any crime in the hood.

Nobody would dare to call them to order because they held keys to the small bioscope then an oasis of entertainment. Those who would have crossed their paths would not be allowed to come for television viewing.

Those who had unlimited access extended to them, did so upon paying in cash and kind. The have-nots television wise, were required to spoil their hosts with some goodies at school especially at break time. That pact that was never written, but was understood by all and sundry grew up in the ghetto during those days. Children who hailed from poor families were given a lifeline when Boka Group of Companies opened a state of the art shopping complex in Dangamvura in the late 80s.

A clique of my hangers on from marginalised families and I used to hang around at the then newly opened Boka Shopping Complex.

The complex, which is situated near Dangamvura High School, Dangamvura Beit Hall and Neighbourhood Tavern, was fixed with five colour television sets, which were all connected to a central Video Cassette Recorder (VCR).

We got to watch videos like Thriller by Michael Jackson, Leonard Dembo's Sharai, Brenda Fassie's It's Nice To Be With People, Weekend Special, Pat Shange's Anytime Babie, Sipho Hotstix Mabuse's Burn Out and others.

Yvonne Chaka Chaka's Thank You Mr DJ, Madonna, Kool and The Gang, Whitney Houston, Tina Turner' What's Love, Bob Dylan, Randy Crawford's Knocking On The Heaven's Door, Queen, Atlantic Star's Silver Shadow and Secret Lovers and Baby Jane rocked us.

Bob Marley's Stir It Up, No Woman No Cry, Buffalo Soldier, I Shot The Sheriff, Peter Tosh's The Poor Man Feel It, Gregory Isaacs' Private Beach Party, Night Nurse, I Wish You Were Mine and Lionel Ritchie's All Night Long as well as some wrestling encounters kept us engrossed on the small boxes. By then we had moved closer to Dangamvura at a quarry were we occupied an abandoned block of houses. That block had been abandoned and vandalised at the height of the liberation struggle. Mudhara then was firmly back in control of the family.

Everyone had forgiven him for his uncalled for behaviour or misdemeanours. Who were we not to have forgiven him when Amai who had struggled to fend for us, had resolved to smoke the peace pipe and accepted him back as her husband and the father of her children? After all, we were only, but fruits of their tempestuous union.

Mudhara had landed as a job as an office orderly and cook at Nazareth Clinic now Sakubva District Hospital. To augment his pittance of a wage, Mudhara would siphon some essential drugs, which were always in short supply from the clinic's dispensary. He would then sell those drugs to desperate patients. He would sometimes use those drugs as bait to win the hearts of fraught women.

He would wink at the women he would have lusted for, conniving with them to come and collect the drugs from his house as soon as their husbands had gone to work. That was exactly what Mudhara used to. To supplement Mudhara's meagre wage, Amai would sell kachasu to the quariers as well as those from surrounding areas. I recall some workers from the company like Masirivha, Dhaimondi, Paundi, Sande, Furaidheyi, Maikoro, Maidhona, Dhonatio, Ginatsiyo, Modhireki, Sitaira, Ferekesi, Firimoni, Charisi, Kirisitofa and two blast men who were known as Tsoko and Jokoniya who would drink like fish.

Even Mbuya Fokofo, a middle-aged lady who would call anyone who would have crossed her path *fokofo*, fuck-off, drank like a fish and she would always swim home after a drinking binge.

Mbuya Musutu and Mbuya Chionini who had gained notoriety for their lose tongues that spewed obscenities, were also hard drinkers. The duo could match any man when it came to drinking contests. They did not get high with ordinary kachasu, but would only show signs of drunkenness whenever they downed the highly intoxicating first brand of the illicit brew known in the beer parlance as *musoro*, the head.

Musoro's alcohol content could have been around fifty percent. It was highly inflammable like petrol and legend had it that it could be used to fuel vehicles. Staying at the quarry had some of its cons.

We had to vacate the block of barracks that we called home whenever the blastmen shouted, *'Hokoyo madhora.'* We would only return home after the last explosion. The blastmen would always tell us the number of blasts or explosions that they would have wired for detonation.

Whenever we returned home, we would listen to Jokoniya the blastman's oasis of tales from the liberation war. The gangly Jokoniya who walked with a limp claimed to have been a member of the Rhodesian Front Army.

He would entertain us with some blood curdling wartime adventures. He would tell us about how he got his leg shot, amputated and replaced with that of a colleague who had been shot dead earlier on in the battle.

He would tell us that, *'Gumbo refu iri harizi rangu, ndere mumwe muface wangu akapfurwa muhondo.'* We would believe him in our youthfulness.

We were so naïve to believe such tales. I would keep Jokoniya and other kachasu imbibers entertained with music, which I played on Bhudhi Mairosi's Supersonic radio.

I was not aware that my family was operating a shebeen neither was I aware of the fact that Amai was the shebeen queen, Mudhara a shebeen king and I, a shebeen disc jockey.

I still vividly recall how one imbiber gallantly and expertly thrashed the living daylights out of Mudhara after he could not take lightly to his comments which he had unknowingly passed on the behind *assets* of the shebeen queen, Amai.

Bhudhi Maikoro and I joined in the fray, fighting in Mudhara's corner. When the imbiber realised that the tables were turning fast and furious, he drew an okapi knife, which he threatened to stab us with. Sensing danger, we made peace and swiftly buried our hatchets. Those were occupational hazards of operating a shebeen.

The country then overflowed with talented DJs like Lazarus Tembo, Hilton Mambo, Itai Godfrey Muchada, Joe Panganai Mukaronda, Patrick Deans Mutume, our own Fungai Marange, Hosiah Singende and Tichafa Matambanadzo.

James Makamba, Kimble Rogers, Nyasha Maphosa-Madzingira, Simon Parkinson, Alice Chavunduka, Lawrence *Bhonzo* Simbarashe, Kelvin Sifelani to mention, but a few who would keep our ear buds throbbing with good sounds. Radio stations then sounded out of this world, good and refreshing.

Live football commentary sounded so live that we could enjoy the live commentaries as if we were at the stadia. We would celebrate with those at various stadia.

We were part and parcel of the game despite the distance. We would weep with our heroes whenever our favourite teams were beaten.

We cried with Evans Mambara that unforgettable night when a super charged Jean Claude Bokande who grabbed a hat trick inside three minutes leaving our boys trailing 3-0 to Senegal tore our Warriors to shreds.

'How this Jean-Claude Bokande can score three goals in three minutes, I wonder?' Cried a spellbound Mambara in Dakar. Those were the days of the great Gabby Mutombo of the Real Sounds of Africa, a group that had migrated from the then Zaire just to make music in Harare.

The group made a name for itself when it released Dynamos Versus Tornadoes, a song that featured a recorded live English commentary of the duel by Charles Mabika.

Those were the days of State House Tornadoes that had the likes of Kuni Matambanadzo, Noah Cox, Peter Gogoma, Fanuel Ariberto, Pasanduka Pakamisa, Jonah *Zvigubhu* Tasanangurwa, Sebastian *Kojak* Chikwature, David *Chikwama* Mwanza, Dadirai Dube, Godfrey Paradza, Forbes Ndaba and Allan Jalasi.

Dynamos featured such greats like Lucky *Dubs* Dube, Ernest *Mr Cool* Mutano, Misheck *Scania* and Sunday Marimo, Oliver *Monitoring Force* Kateya and Edward *Madhobha-Twinkle Toes* Katsvere, David *Yogi* Mandigora, July *Juju* Sharara, Moses *Razorman* and Kembo Chunga, Kuda *Kuda Boy* Muchemeyi and Kenneth *The Computer* Jere.

The scintillating league encounter that was played at Gwanzura Stadium ended in a three-all stalemate.

Mutombo did another scorcher of a soccer song that featured Dynamos and Caps United. Sunday Marimo – Dynamos, Shacky Tauro – Kepekepe, Kuda Muchemeyi – Dynamos, Anthony Kambani – Kepe Kepe, Lucky Dube – Dynamos, Size Torindo – Kepe Kepe.

That was Dynamos and Tornadoes for you, a team that was too good to be relegated. That was Caps United for you, a team that burst to the seams with talent.

That was real soccer for you. That was real live soccer commentary for you, commentaries that swept us off our feet. Those were the days when we would keep some soccer books. We would cut and paste pictures of our favourite footballers from The Herald, The Sunday Mail, The Weekly, Parade, Horizon, Prize Beat, Prize

Africa and Moto magazines into our soccer books. We would read some incisive soccer reports by sports reporters of the likes of Jahoor Omar, Allan Hlatshwayo, Sam Marisa, Tendai Ndemera, Sam Mawokomatanda, Collin Matiza and Peter Gwinyai.

CHAPTER 19

THE PERPETUAL LIE

During the weekends, we would also make some sleeping mats, *maponde enhokwe*, which Amai would sell in Dangamvura. She would have fetched the nhokwe from Rimai Farm or kwaKonde near the border with Mozambique.

Amai was very strict. She would set some targets for us during the weekends. By that time, we had moved from the quarry to a nearby farm.

We would get to be released only after we would have crafted together two mats a day. We would be engaged in money games, which featured our team from the farm and an array of teams from Dangamvura.

Our well-oiled and youthful team, in which David and I were the only big boys, would never lose a match. I would play both the central defence and central midfield whilst Deaver would play the attacking midfield and central striker's role.

Deaver, who attended Mutanda Primary in Sakubva, was a long-time friend. The two of us had first met when we sojourned at a Rural Road Department near Blue Desert.

We had sported oversized uniforms that our parents believed we would grow up in them.

Deaver revolved to be our team's mainstay, our trump card and pivotal man. He carried our hopes on his shoulders. He was blessed with some exquisite dribbling, ball juggling skills as well as an eye for goal.

He took his football seriously whilst I sometimes would revert to taking part in some unisex traditional games like dhere, dunhu, chuti, lakalaka, tsetsetse or pada. Deaver would take some football bladders, wrap them over with a number of empty roller meal packets so as to give the ball a bouncy effect.

Those balls would make some rival teams from Dangamvura turn green with envy. I recall vividly when I almost killed Razaro *Madhora*, one of my friends from a rival team that hailed from the quarry.

Madhora had swept past me and being the last man in that sole man rear-guard, I had no choice, but to hack him down from behind.

He fell awkwardly and struck his head against a hard ground. He picked himself up, staggered and plunged on to the pitch before drifting into some convulsions and hallucinations.

Play had to be stopped as our hearts skipped a bit. After the convulsions, he went limb and gave out a sigh as if he had breathed his last. For the next ten minutes, we all watched him as he appeared to have drifted into his final journey to his Maker. Someone, somewhere in the spiritual real must have had turned low his lights of consciousness. After ten minutes, he came around and asked for a swig of water from me, which I hesitantly offered him.

I was afraid that I might have given him his last swig. He tugged at the water container and gulped mouthfuls of water as if his life depended on that precious liquid. After those swigs, beads of sweat formed on his forehead before cascading down his entire body leaving him drenched to the bone.

We all heaved huge sighs of relief despite the fact that he appeared to have lost some of his memory. He did not know what had happened to him. We called off the match and I accompanied the groggy Madhora home.

It took him two full days to recuperate to his former self. From that day onwards, I never tackled anybody. I had evolved to become a technically sound and smart player as I sought to shake off the tough tackler tag that I had earned.

During the night, Amai would require us to make strings from fibres. Again, we would only retire to bed once we would have attained set targets.

Bhudhi Maikoro who then was about to sit for his Ordinary Level, would be spared from the rigours of string making as well as mat crafting. His job was to prepare sisal fibre, which we would yarn into strings on our legs.

That business would leave those who were hairy without hair. All the mats that we would have crafted, would be sold by Amai during the week. That enabled us to eat good food as well as dress decently even though I still sported some patched shorts.

I would detest being sent to Dangamvura for shopping in those patched shorts. I would rather put on my school uniform short than be a laughing stock among my peers from Dangamvura.

I did not want my classmates or schoolmates to know that we were staying at Manyandure Farm near D & E Crushers.

Even during our stint at the now defunct quarry, I would not pluck up enough courage to tell my classmates where I dwelled at. Doing so would have earned me nicknames such as *Madhora, Pinto* or *Kwari*.

That would have taken my educational focus off its stride. I would lie to all my mates that I stayed in Fern Valley and that earned me some respect among my peers. When it came to addresses, I had no problem with that.

I had partly grown up in that neighbourhood before independence. After independence, we used to roam that hood in search of mushrooms that we would hawk to augment cash for Christmas goodies.

In a nutshell, I was familiar with the suburb like the back of my hand. Trouble started around 1985 when the school got a Deputy Head who hailed from that neighbourhood.

I remembered one day when he got into our classroom, the very day he was introduced to us. He mentioned that he lived in Fern Valley and our teacher swiftly made it known to him that I also hailed from that hood. He started to ask me where I stayed and my surname.

I told him my surname and he confidently told all those who cared to listen that there was nobody with such a name who owned a plot in Fern Valley. To save face, I told him that we were tenants at an address that I had given him. That drew many giggles from some of my classmates.

I hated that administrator for almost succeeding in blowing up my cover. I had to keep my distance from him in case he might bump into our imaginary landlord. That was the problem with a lie. It had to be told and lived times without a number for it to hold water.

A lie that I had lived with for more than five years, a lie that I had told times without number almost got me exposed for who I really was. I had to perfect that lie, tie any loose ends so that I kept it under wraps.

Nobody dared to investigate me or challenge me to own up with regards with my place of residence because I always top scored for my class and grade. That endeared me with teachers who conferred me with a prefect status.

I became one of the most sought after pupils at the school, with girls. Girls would flock to me wanting to ride on my fame, which was brought by my intelligence. I later enrolled at Elise Gledhill in Sakubva for my secondary education. I would walk to Elise Gledhill from the farm.

The school then was synonymous with rare football talent and students thin on academic prowess. Even though I had a short stint in Sakubva before, I would always brook whenever threatened with physical harm with ghetto youths.

I had heard a lot of ghoulish tales from this hood, tales that always sent chills down my spine. After all, I was never brought up in a hood whose inhabitants would always ride on their shenanigans to instil fear into weaker aliens.

'Haikona kuda kutamba ndini uri kuzwa ere? Ndiri born remuSakubva.'

That statement alone would send the jelly kneed into a wobbly trance. I spent the first two months of my form one without a uniform.

I would put on a pair of shorts from Sheni Primary, a matching brown or rather coffee t-shirt passed onto me from Bhudhi Mairosi who had enlisted into the National Parks and Wildlife, six years back.

I would match that with a pair of North Star doled out to me by Sisi Gaudhenziya. I continued to peddle that lie of mine that unfortunately had become part of my DNA.

My former classmates and schoolmates from Sheni Primary would blindly vouch for me. I continued to excel in my academics and nobody dared to question my attire, which all things being equal should have given me away. After school, I would team up with other boys from D & E Crushers and squatters from Mudhabura Farm in raiding some primary school children off their sadza cakes, makoko at Mutare Teachers' College.

Makoko then were a delicacy. To spice the makoko we would steal some Stock or Buttercup margarine from home, which we would spread on the makokos.

In no time, I had recruited a number of boys from my school who hailed from Dangamvura's Area 13 and 14. They too fell in love with makoko. We would walk through Dangamvura water reservoirs. We would get to separate whenever I branched off to my place of residence Fern Valley.

As time flirted by, Mudhara bought me my first secondary school uniform. That uniform enabled me to blend well with fellow students. Unfortunately, I did not have a satchel and continued to stuff my books in plastic shopping bags. These were a bit stronger and durable. They too should have given my doctored background away.

Chapter 20

Rumour from the Underworld

My breakthrough or gateway out of perpetual poverty, *kuponda nhamo*, came in the late 80s when Bhudhi Maikoro who had spurned a chance to enrol for his Advanced Level at the then prestigious Mutare Boys High School in 1986, landed an apprenticeship place at the National Railways of Zimbabwe.

At then one of Mutare's leading lights in terms of remuneration, he learnt the ropes of Diesel Plant Fitting.

Even during those days as a Trainee Artisan, he earned money that turned most civil servants green with envy. And do you know what Bhudhi Maikoro and one of his best friends Alexander used to do to bait ladies they would have fallen for?

They would deliberately drop their fat payslips in front of those ladies. They would take time to pick those payslips to enable their targets ample time to scan through the figures. Sometimes the trick would work, but at times, it did not.

At the end of 1988, Bhudhi Maikoro who had cheated death a number of times after running into snares by some thugs who waylaid people who used the Dora Pinto road, decided to relocate to Dangamvura's Area 13. Bhudhi Maikoro was a night crawler, a joy seeker. Surely, having grown up in a family that reeked with poverty who would have blamed him?

He would take me to some night gigs. I remember attending my first musical show in the late 80s. I was still at primary school when he took me to Jonah Moyo's show that took place at Dangamvura Beit Hall.

He later took me to another musical gig dubbed 'Live at Sakubva' that was hosted by Oliver M'tukudzi when he recorded the country's first live show recording.

Bhudhi Maikoro invited me to stay with him at his lodgings. Bhudhi Mairosi and his heavily pregnant wife Amaiguru Rottinna had earlier on moved to Chikanga, a suburb whose residential stands had just been parcelled out.

Bhudhi Rotario and his wife, the party spoiler Amaiguru Roffinna, had moved homes to Zimunya Township on the outskirts of Mutare where her lethal birds allegedly wreaked havoc in the sprawling community.

Bhudhi Rotario would move around badmouthing some members of the community so as to cross their paths. Once that happened, he would enlist the services of the lethal birds.

Amaiguru Roffinna who was always spoiling for both *infantry and aerial fights* would move around the community borrowing money and other stuff, which she would not repay. Once her creditors start to breath down her neck, she would threaten them with unspecified action resulting in the lethal birds descending heavily on whoever would have crossed her path, paths that she would have deliberately created.

She even ended up staying at her lodgings for free as the landlord feared for his life. Money launderers from the community ended up enlisting her services in debt recovery, for a handsome commission of course.

But the gods had spoken or warned Bhudhi Rotario about this beforehand. But who was complaining about Amaiguru Roffinna's nocturnal business? It certainly was not Bhudhi Rotario for he was enjoying the fruits of the lethal birds.

If they were any complaints by members of the family, the complainant had to make sure that the complaint would never reach Amaiguru Roffinna or Bhudhi Rotario's ear. Why raise an issue then when that issue could result in somebody being fast tracked to the graveyard?

Amaiguru Roffinna and Bhudhi Rotario had become untouchables and a law unto themselves. Nobody could dare them in the community. That mentality had also rubbed onto their daughter Ndaiziveyi who had the guts to challenge older contemporaries to bouts of fights.

She would openly brag about her mother's witchcraft prowess. Rumour from the underworld had it that she was voted into the leadership of the witches and wizards association, a black magic grouping.

A black magic grouping where the mere mention of her name would sent shivers down the spine of her colleagues. Mudhara made a historical return to Fern Valley in the late 80s, a hood he had left in the late 70s after his infamous clash with a clique of the racial drugged whites led by Baas Botha.

I would cook, tidy, sweep our room and do Bhudhi Maikoro's laundry whilst he in return would feed, clothe and pay for my school fees. He would take care of my general upkeep. Our living standards improved for the better. Our lives were generally good.

Our diet improved tremendously so did our fashion trends. Bhudhi Maikoro could afford to spoil me with real beef as well as real tinned pork and tinned fish. Bhudhi Maikoro would take me to Meikles and Edgars for shopping.

From Meikles, I chose my first Grasshopper school shoes then a hit with schoolboys from Mutare Boys High School, *Pfacha* and St Dominics High School.

He spruced up my image by buying me another pair of school shorts, another school shirt and a maroon jersey and a James North satchel then known as kit. By then I had transferred to Dangamvura High School. By then the school had evolved and shed off her bad image to become one of Mutare's leading academic lights. He bought a portable double deck radio cassette from which we would listen to music of our time. He would also buy some blank cassettes on which we would dub music being played over the radio. Sometimes we would dub from an original cassette using a double deck radio cassette.

CHAPTER 21

TITANIC CLASHES

Talk of Dangamvura Beit Hall, I still have some gaudy memories of some brilliant football encounters that were played at the Dangamvura Community pitch that stares the hall. We witnessed the crème' de la crème' of football talent from the sprawling suburb.

We witnessed the likes of the Korosiya brothers led by the agile goalie Wonder and the nimble footed Taurai who starred for the now defunct Mutare Board and Paper Mills.

The Simbi brothers Jealous and Barns, Edmore *Beefy* Kapfumvuti, Bokande, Emmanuel Maluwa, Kudzanai *Kwedzu* Kadzirange, Blessing Makunike and the Mutukwa brothers Waxington and Handsome during their formative years.

Teams like Mutare Board and Paper Mills, Flamingo, 32 Infantry Brigade bankrolled Dangamvura United formerly Chaminuka United, Scissors Blade, Gluelam, B & C, Feruka aka CPMZ, UBC aka Zupco Mutare, Manica Hot Sun, Tomango, GMB Coffee to mention, but a few would battle it out for supremacy week in, week out.

Old men from the Two Rooms Section would bring along benches and small chairs on which to sit during the duels. We would vociferously root for our boys, boys from the community who would play their hearts out.

They would strive never to disappoint the multitudes who thronged the community pitch week in, week out. A spitting distance away from the community pitch, young tennis prodigies among them Genius Chidzikwe, Pfungwa Mahepfu, David and Blessing Bvunzawabaya would be sweating it out at the community tennis court, learning the ropes from established mentors like Richmore Murape. That was Dangamvura for you. A neighbourhood that burst to the seams with talent.

This hood was home to the M'parutsas, Peter, the late Fortune, Tendai and Wallace. Tendai Lewis a jazz sensation, ZiFM's duo of Kelvin Jakachira and Chengetai Murimwa, Minister Supa Mandiwanzira, Paul Phiri of the famed Black Saints, Staben Mawire of Chimbekeya fame, revered long distance runners Point Chaza and Charles Soza, former Tanganda United stars Emmanuel Maluwa and

Fordson Chitakatira, cricketer Tendai Chatara and others too numerous to mention.

Some *rowdy* ghetto martial artistes from Sakubva would troop to Dangamvura Beit Hall where they would want to force their way into the venue, thereby disturbing peace and tranquillity.

That would result in bloody fistfights with some martial artistes from Dangamvura who would be out to defend their territory, their pride. Usually those from Sakubva who would be usually outnumbered would quickly retreat into their shells, their hood.

They would avenge that defeat whenever martial artistes from Dangamvura who might have forgotten about the previous skirmish, decided to attend a disco show at Sakubva Beit Hall, their fortress.

I vividly recall how some martial artistes at Musika Wehuku thumped some Form Ones from my stream and school where they had gone to board a Zupco bus back to Dangamvura after classes.

We later learnt that the thumping that only stopped after some martial artistes from Dangamvura resolved to escort the youngsters was ignited by a whitewash defeat that had been suffered by some martial artistes from Sakubva during a disco show at Dangamvura Beit Hall.

So deep was the rivalry, that existed between martial artistes from Dangamvura and Sakubva.

The mere mention of names like Master Mushoriwa Zambuko aka Master Sho; who was widely believed to have had some training stints in China, Master Pension Gwinyai aka Master Pay, Master Lucky Saungweme, Master Charles Sambare, Master Lawrence Kagonegone, Master Juma Wasili, Master Zvingowanisei to mention, but a few would send shivers down our spines.

People who would have been wronged would then hire some of these Masters who were belligerent, to fight on their behalf. They were also used in the recovery of debts that would have been outstanding for long just like Gagan.

The Gagan Brothers were *notorious* for attaching residents' properties. Residents who would have been indebted to others, those who were in the habit of failing to service their debts for whatever reason.

The mere mention of the name Gagan invoked sad memories among bad debtors for most of them were left counting the costs of unfaithfulness.

CHAPTER 22

UNDER SIEGE

Amai, Sisi Tambudzai and three nieces of mine had moved to Mt Darwin's Mukumbura area, after having had enough of the farm life. Amai had to be hosted by Tete Erizabheti during the construction of her homestead.

Two months down the line, she moved into her newly constructed homestead and bade farewell to Tete Erizabheti, the foul-mouthed one.

The motor mouth Tete Erizabheti would tell anyone who cared to listen that she was sick and tired of playing host to a sister-in-law who had chosen to follow her husband to the big city instead of braving the raging flame of the Second Chimurenga War.

As fate would have it, a civil war was escalating in neighbouring Mozambique. And Zimbabwe who had been hosted by the Frelimo government presided over by Cde Samora Machel during the protracted Second Chimurenga war, had to come to the aid of her all weather neighbour by intervening militarily.

That led to the routing of Renamo bandits under Alfonso Dhlakama at bases such as Cassa Banana and Gorongoza. Lt Col Dyke of the famed Sixth Brigade, led in the destruction of the Renamo rebels who were ironically trained and armed by the Smith regime at Odzi, just outside Mutare.

Stung by massive loses and a dithering stronghold, the Renamo rebels turned their anger and frustrations against Zimbabwean civilians who lived along the border with Mozambique.

A number of Zimbabweans in Chipinge, Mukumbura, Burma Valley's Mapofu area, Stappleford, Honde Valley and Pfunyanguwo were mutilated, killed, maimed, women and girls sexually assaulted by the insurgents. Others had their homes torched by the rebels. The Zimbabwe Defence Forces swiftly moved in to protect their compatriots. After supper, civilians were required to assemble at schools where they would sleep under guard from the army.

That siege by Renamo rebels took away a bit of the civilians' freedom. A number of civilians who had survived the brutality of the Renamo bandits, relocated to safer zones.

Amai who had become tired of being harangued by the fear of Renamo rebels or Matsanga, resolved to relocate to Mudzengerere village near the famed Karanda Mission Hospital.

Mudhara and Bhudhi Maikoro pooled their resources together and bought a stand that comprised of a two-roomed house and a round hut kitchen. The army in Mukumbura and other troubled spots finally restored peace. Nevertheless, Amai decided to stay put in her new village, far from the madding Tete Erizabheti who constantly laid siege on her, tearing at her at will.

To Amai, the Renamo incursions into Mukumbura had come as a blessing in disguise. She just could not withstand both the sight and vitriol of Tete Erizabheti. I would visit Amai, Sisi Tambudzai and the three nieces of mine, over the school holidays.

The trio had dropped out of school due to financial constraints. The other sister of mine Porina had eloped with a member of the Zimbabwe Paramilitary Army whose members were recruited from the ruling party's youths.

Party youths then wore red shirts and khaki trousers with matching black berets, *mabhareta*. Back then youths who were older, muscular, brawnier than we were, took great pride in sporting those fatigues.

The likes of Differed, Power, Noise, Message, Defeat, Pabva Bango Pasekesa, Kasikipa, Mapfirikiti and Dedza Wanzvera looked like members of the Korean trained paramilitary unit. We always envied them.

Chapter 23

The Preferred Choice

When school holidays were over, I would fly to Mutare via Harare. Back in Mutare, I would visit Mudhara in Fern Valley armed with that double deck radio cassette. I would walk to Fern Valley via Mamenemuno Farm through thick bushes blasting music of our time.

In one hand, I would be dangling the musical spitting machine whilst in the other, I would be holding on to a pen on which to rewind cassettes with.

Those in the know would tell you that rewinding and fast forwarding of cassettes on the decks had the effect of draining power from batteries, torch cells. Later Bhudhi Maikoro and I moved to the Zesa compound in Dangamvura's Area 14. We would buy bread and other items from some tuckshops known then as *zvibheka*, some of which were made from some dilapidated scooters or tricycle motor bikes. There was one enterprising tuckshop operator John Baker, who had stood the test of time.

We used to buy from his well-stocked tuckshop during our stints at the quarry and Manyandure Farm. At the end of 1990, Bhudhi Maikoro qualified as a Diesel Plant Fitter.

He together with the likes of friends like Russell and Richard among others were placed in a cage at Meikles Park. The appies cum artisans were immersed in black grease turning them into grotesque or silhouette figures.

It was a frightening spectacle to those alien to the trade, but a cherished spectacle to the would-be journeyman.

The young men's journey in the Diesel and Plant Fitting, the artisan world had just begun. After that historical, momentous, monumental and moving occasion, some would pack their toolboxes and embark on a journey into the real world.

Others, who would be sceptical of what the future might hold for them, would stick around with the company. And stick around with the company, Bhudhi Maikoro, Russell and Richard did.

That same year, he bought a better radio from Pelhams Store, A Supersonic Chesterfield 3. That one could rival the one that used to be owned by Mujubheki back in the 70s.

Bhudhi Maikoro was better off than Mujubheki because he had bought the radio, a sophisticated remake of the gramophone without having migrated to Wenera or Joni as Johannesburg then was affectionately and fondly referred to by migrants.

At the end of 1990, he married his childhood sweetheart Amaiguru Furorenzi from Florida, once a coloured community in the mould of Arcadia and Braeside.

She moved in with us in February 1991 after all the traditional rites were performed under the watchful eye of Sekuru Makombe who had been taking instructions from Mudhara and Amai.

When Amaiguru Furorenzi joined us, she sought to change the appearance of the two rooms that we rented. By then we had moved down to the heart of Area 14. She sought to give the rented rooms a feminine touch, a feminine class, a ladylike look.

Amaiguru Furorenzi persuaded Bhudhi Maikoro to purchase a four-piece Kensington lounge suit from Pelhams.

Chapter 24

A Status Symbol

We later moved further down Area 14 near Nyamauru High where we occupied a full house, a three roomed core house referred to then as *tumaZvobgo*. The core houses were built during Dr Eddison Zvobgo's reign as Housing Minister.

Amaiguru determined to give our house, a homely appearance and feminine touch went on to purchase a kitchen dresser, a colour television set and a kitchen table. Kitchen dressers then were known as kitchen units.

She went on to improve out diet. She would buy Lacto, which she would mix with creamy milk to give it a creamier and tastier taste.

On Saturdays, we would enjoy breakfast served with bread that would have been toasted with eggs. She also sought to improve the family's wardrobe.

She bought me my first pair of jeans, my first pair of glass shoes as well as my second pair of Adidas snickers when I was in my final year of my Ordinary Level studies.

After coming out with impressive results in my Ordinary Level exams, I could not proceed to Advanced Level let alone enrol with any tertiary institution since I had not realised the importance of such a move. After all, we were never invited for career guidance symposiums. If it were today, I would have chosen a better career that would have taken me elsewhere

Unfortunately, I never did and still regret why I could not choose a marketable profession. Had I chosen a marketable profession then, I would have been somewhere soaring with the eagles.

I failed to realise my potential and that has since heavily impacted on my life, my career and family. I am still under siege from abject poverty having failed to wean myself from its clutches.

In 1994, I landed a Motor Mechanics Apprenticeship with a leading car-repairing dealer in Mutare, Dulys. I learnt the ropes of the trade under the watchful eyes of our team of foremen. I graduated as an Artisan after a gruelling three years of apprenticeship in which I earned enough money to pay for my upkeep as well as Amai. The company could not absorb all of us and armed with our Journeyman Class One certificates, we journeyed off in search of greener pastures.

I ended up landing a job with Redwing Mine, a gold mining concern just outside Mutare. I was offered accommodation that was commensurate with my position, a Junior Motor Mechanic.

Two years later, I married my childhood sweetheart Rangarirai who I had kept in my mind. I had kept our promise and had stuck to our childhood vow, a vow that we had made whilst playing house. We began a new life, a new family with in-laws and extended families as well as new responsibilities. We were venturing into new territories, into an unknown jungle. When I got married to Rangarirai, she had dropped out of school after sitting for her Junior Certificate due to a financial quagmire. She had to work as a domestic worker for a number of professional couples.

She would use her meagre earnings to send her brothers to school, a role she played with distinction, zeal and zest hoping to be repaid both in cash and in kind in the near future. I took over her role in putting her three brothers through university.

Two of them graduated with Law degrees whilst the other graduated with a General Medical Practitioner degree.

After securing employment, I was of the opinion that the trio would fend for their parents as well as their two sisters' educational needs, but alas that was not to be. They turned their backs on the family including my wife and I.

I was shattered. All my hopes of getting a relief were shattered into shrapnel. I had to continue with the payment of school fees for my two sisters-in-law whom I stayed with up to tertiary college.

One trained as a Human Resources Manager at Mutare Polytechnic College whilst the other trained as a secondary school teacher at Mutare Teachers' College. Upon realising that I would never recoup anything for my efforts, I proposed love to them.

At first, the duo turned my proposals down. The pair had to rescind on their decisions after I threatened to withdraw my funding. That was way back in 1997 when the Economic Structural Adjustment Programme, ESAP, had just been introduced in Zimbabwe on the instigation of the International Monetary Fund.

Thousands of Zimbabweans were made redundant with very little in terms of severance or retrenchment packages. The programme threatened to reverse the gains of independence. The Zimbabwe

Congress of Trade Unions called for crippling strikes and mass stay aways.

I started to bed my two sisters-in-law alternating them with my wife whom I was beginning to treat as a rag due to her poor educational background. My sisters-in-law, Diana and Daisy, had swept me off my feet.

I became closer to Daisy and Diana than to my wife Rangarirai. She began to suspect my movements.

CHAPTER 25

WAGES OF SIN

One Friday afternoon she lied to me that she would be visiting Amaiguru Furorenzi and Babamukuru Maikoro in Dangamvura where she would spend the weekend. She took along our then three-year-old daughter Nakai.

I saw that as a perfect opportunity to satisfy my insatiable sexual appetite. After work, I went to a call box and phoned Mainini Daisy from Mutare Poly to come over for the weekend and she dully obliged.

I could have driven to town to pick her up with my rickety Peugeot 504 station wagon, which was inscribed with the spiteful words, *'Getekete Ndimhayi wako, tevera tione.'*

Indeed, that jalopy of mine that emitted a lot of carbon monoxide, which impacted negatively on the ozone layer, was a spent force.

When Amainini Daisy arrived around six in the evening, I was busy in the kitchen preparing a dinner for two. I had planned a surprise candle-lit dinner for the two of us. Amainini Daisy was not comfortable with the arrangement. She had a premonition that her elder sister would pounce on us. I assured her that nothing of that sort was going to happen.

She felt at ease and became high after I spiked her soft drink with a drug. After having enjoyed the candlelit dinner, we started to regale and fox trotted on the dance floor like Romeo and Juliet.

When we retired to the matrimonial bed, both of us were stone drunk. I committed adultery with Amainini Daisy. We had done it before on countless occasions elsewhere, but not the matrimonial bed.

We had taken our amorous affair to another level, a dangerous one to be precise. We later slept soundly like infants in each other's arms.

The following day, a Saturday, we spent the entire day indoors and exploring each other's bodies. We just could not get enough of each other.

Nobody could sense that it was a bad omen. After another

candlelit dinner and another round of amorous assault, our attention was drawn by a squeaking sound of a door followed by the pattering of feet.

Before I could get dressed, so that I could investigate the source of the sound, my wife with the baby Nakai strapped to her back, stood on the doorway of our bedroom. She was perplexed by what she had seen.

Her beautiful younger sister Daisy slept soundly on my chest, spent, paralysed, hypotenused and drugged with love. I tried to explain myself but nothing came out.

Angrily Rangarirai banged the bedroom door, locked it from outside and vanished. Moments later, she was back armed with a pot full of boiling cooking oil, which she hurled at us.

I leapt and landed awkwardly on the floor badly dislocating my pelvic girdle in the process. Daisy was not swift enough. She met the full wrath of the cooking oil that scalded her beautiful face instantly turning it into a shrivelled mess.

Her breasts were not spared from the instant justice by a jealousy and insecure wife. She let out a scream that threw the entire compound into a panic mode if not in a quandary.

In a few minutes, the whole compound was milling around our house. A hullabaloo had flared up like a volcano, spewing words like lava.

Amainini Daisy was rushed to a local clinic from where she was immediately transferred to Mutare Provincial Hospital where she was treated for first-degree burns.

The police picked up Rangarirai. A warned and cautioned statement was recorded from her. Another warned and cautioned statement was also recorded from me.

Rangarirai was held at Mutare Remand Prison where she awaited to be charged with the most appropriate charge upon Amainini Daisy's discharge from hospital.

My in-laws who were furious with my actions, came and took away Nakai from my custody. Rangarirai had committed a heinous crime of passion whilst the once beautiful Daisy, an oasis of beauty during her heydays or rather prior to the unfortunate and callous attack by her heartless sister, lay in the Burns Ward where she battled for her precious life.

They squarely blamed me for having driven a wedge between

their daughters. What angered them most was the fact that Daisy had been diagnosed with a three months old pregnancy, which was attributed to me.

When Diana visited Daisy in hospital, she immediately threw up. She was also taken ill, admitted and later underwent a pregnancy test. She also tested positive after undergoing a pregnancy test. I was also responsible for her pregnancy.

Rangarirai was also heavily pregnant with our second child. I had to be hospitalised at Mutare's Seventh Avenue Surgical Unit (SASU), which then was an upmarket private clinic where I battled to recuperate from my pelvic girdle dislocation.

I was discharged from the hospital after two months. Even though I had recovered from the effects of the awkward fall, it left a permanent limping gait in my step. I still walk with a limp, a constant reminder of my todos. I had paid dearly for my infidelity with a physical condition that I have failed to shrug off. Amainini Daisy was later discharged from the hospital after three months.

Her face remained a scarecrow even after grafting, a constant reminder of the wages of sin. She suffered a miscarriage due to a plethora of psychological effects brought by her condition. She had to be deferred at college. Rangarirai was later sentenced to an effective 18 months after the same number of months were slashed down for being a first offender.

Chapter 26

Mitigation

Her attempted murder charge was commuted to a lesser charge of culpable homicide after all her mitigation and extenuating circumstances were taken into consideration. She later gave birth to a bouncy baby boy Muchadura at Mutare Prison Farm where she did her time.

Diana also gave birth to a baby boy Muchatongwa. She had to drop out of college to nurse our baby. I was forced by my in-laws to take both Diana and Daisy in as my lawful wives.

My brother in-laws who could not stomach how I had torn their family apart, constantly came to my work place to physically assault me. I was given broken ribs during one of their raids.

I was hospitalised for close to two months at SASU. Upon my release from the house of mend, the clinic, I resumed my duties at Redwing Mine.

The heavy battering that I constantly suffered at the hands of my rabid and livid brothers in-law impacted negatively on my work performance. The company had no choice, but to terminate my contract on the grounds of incompetence.

By then, I was heavily saddled with debts. I was literally swimming in tempestuous waters of debts in which I was struggling to stay afloat or keep my head above water level. I was slowly sinking in debt. I paid off some debts by my terminal benefits. Three months later, I vacated the company house and relocated to Sakubva where I occupied a makeshift timber cottage in the Chisamba Singles Section known in the sprawling ghetto as Japan. That was way back in 2004.

To eke a living, I had to use my old jalopy as a pirate taxi. By then, Rangarirai had re-joined us from prison. She was released on medical grounds after prison authorities had realised that her health was failing. She and our son Muchadura were battling with tuberculosis, which she had contracted in prison.

A month after Rangarirai's release, we lost Muchadura who had succumbed to a recurring bout of pneumonia. I could not afford to foot Muchadura's funeral bills. A Councillor for our ward as well as wellwishers from our community donated in cash and kind towards

Muchadura's funeral. Before I could recover from Muchadura's departure, his mother surrendered in to her battle against tuberculosis.

It was crystal clear that Rangarirai would not win her battle no matter how brave she would have loved to soldier on. The *crime drugged community* of Chisamba Singles had to come to my aid once more.

During Rangarirai's funeral wake, I had to weep uncontrollably when I overheard a neighbour speaking on his mobile phone.

I heard the neighbour poignantly saying, *'Muface wangu ndiri pafinaz yechirema, chikumbodai chekumaraini kwangu chevakadzi gozha chamadhirwa newaifazi yacho hombe yanga iri kuzandomu.'*

Because of lust and lack of self-control, my life had fallen from grace to disgrace. Because of lust and an open zip policy, my life that had been the envy of many of my contemporaries, had fallen off the radar of progress and prosperity.

Because of lust, I had become a laughing stock, a societal misfit, the poverty stricken community's biblical Lazarus, a beggar who once prowled a beach of gold that I had failed to utilise.

Because of my myopic judgment or rushed decisions, I had gone through from being a provider to a recipient of alms even from the poorest in the community. Because of lust, I was slowly sliding into oblivion, obscurity out of existence and out of sight.

Even my intimate relatives and bosom buddies seemed to have abandoned me in my times of need. They all appeared to have given up on me for I had messed up big time.

All and sundry had washed their hands on me. They had Pontius Pilatoed on my destiny. They all appeared to have resigned everything to fate.

They had placed my fate and destiny into the hands of the Creator. There were some who biblically believed that I was being punished for my transgression, my sins. I had sinned and so had everyone. *We are all sinners, aren't we? Who hasn't sinned anyway? Who among us can claim to be a perfectionist?* Rangarirai had to be kept at the mortuary for close to a month, as my in-laws demanded their outstanding lobola dues.

They had vowed that they would not have her entombed until the last outstanding cent of the lobola had been paid.

I ran around with a begging bowl as I desperately tried to save the situation. Friends and relatives would slam their doors shut in my face whenever I darkened their doors. I had been borrowing and borrowing from them until I ended up borrowing the word borrow.

They had all concurred that I was no longer a candidate who could be loaned out some money. I was swimming in a black pool of debts. I was groping in a dungeon of despair.

I was waddling in puddles of debts that had left me stinking and sinking. I was battling to stay afloat. Even some straws that I desperately tried to clutch to were no longer on my side.

They too had abandoned me and snapping at an alarming rate and were giving in. The centre could no longer hold. Things were falling apart like a deck of cards.

I no longer had any card that I kept closer to my chest. I no longer had an ace, which I could pull out. The devil had pulled a fast one on me. The devil had pulled the rug right under my feet.

The devil who I thought I had befriended when I went on a spree of devilish shenanigans had abandoned me leaving me soaked under a deluge of tears.

The devil had left me listening to some echoes and encores of his raucous laughter. After all, the horned one had his mission accomplished. With no help in sight and my landlord stepping on my toes, I had no choice, but to dispose of my old jalopy on which my struggling family relied for their survival.

I used proceeds from the sale of the jalopy to try to offset the lobola debt. The proceeds were not enough. They fell short of the debt having been consumed by a raging inflation rate, a galloping one, the worst in living memory.

Rangarirai's parents could not agree to bury their daughter even after having paid them with proceeds from the sale of my jalopy.

Tired of their endless and unreasonable demands, I had to engage Sakubva Police Station's Public Relations Department. They only agreed to lay their daughter to rest following a series of meetings coupled with threats of arrest.

CHAPTER 27

THE POST-MORTEM

My illiterate in-laws were not aware of the fact that by refusing to give their daughter a befitting send-off and decent burial, they were violating her rights and were therefore committing a crime.

'What rights? Do the dead have rights?' They had asked captivated. When she was finally laid to rest, the funeral wake had plummeted to a family gathering. The send-off resembled that of a pauper.

My in-laws later forced me to consult n'angas and prophets to find out the cause of deaths of Rangarirai and Muchadura. This in our Shona custom is known as *gata*.

At first, I refused to accompany them on their witch hunting missions. I only complied when they threatened to invoke the spirits of the duo to rise against me.

We visited a prophet and two n'angas who all pointed to Amaiguru Roffinna who they accused of having sent her zvishiri to strike the pair over a long-standing family feud.

To authenticate those claims, the trio that is the prophet and two sangomas, commanded the spirits of the departed to manifest which they did. The voice of Amaiguru Roffinna could be heard loud and clear. The spiritual healers all agreed to invoke the spirits of the deceased to rise against Amaiguru Roffinna.

Three months later, I was served with an eviction notice since I was no longer able to pay for my rentals. Within those three months, the local government issued an ultimatum to all urban dwellers to demolish all illegal structures including wooden makeshift housing cabins.

The game was up. Nobody took the ultimatum seriously until the very day the ultimatum lapsed. We woke up in a pre-dawn siege from the no nonsense riot police known in the police parlance as *Gondo Harishayi*.

Legend has it that whenever an eagle misses its target usually a chick, it will clutch onto some rubbish.

The sprawling suburb woke up from the big deep sleep of the Creator under siege from the combative riot officers who were backed by the dog section and menacing water canon vans ready to spring into action should residents resort to militant tactics.

We swiftly salvaged what we deemed valuable assets before the wooden cabins were demolished to the ground. The neighbourhood was plunged into Sodom and Gomorrah as smoke billowed and belched from *assets*, which had suddenly been condemned as excess baggage.

I scrunched for some leftovers of assets, which I loaded into a pushcart, which wheeled what was left of my once jealously guarded *assets* to Musika Wehuku where I intended to board a kombi to quary.

My two wives were against the idea of squatting at the derelict and abandoned compound houses. But then we were not spoilt for choice. We were beggars who could not be offered the option of a choice.

Some of the compound houses that had wings and yawning orifices for windows, appeared vandalised, haunted and inhabitable. Their roofs curved outwards, *misana yenzou*.

The roofs were draped and dripped with a shiny silver colour, were made of concrete slabs. Only ghosts could live in them.

In order to live in those houses, which were cold in winters and very steamy hot during summer, we took to phantom like features and characters.

The haunted houses belonged to no one, but the Pintos of Florida who owned the land on which the quarry was situated. Nobody could claim rentals for the desolated houses.

This was a scenario that favoured my family since we were frantic and hovering into the destitute's drop zone. We were waddling into the murky waters of destitute.

We had no roof over our heads. We were vagabonds and beggars who had once sat on a beach of gold. There was nothing to show that we had once rubbed shoulders, shared lip-smacking dishes and beverages as well as exchanging notes with the who is who of Mutare. There was nothing to show that I was once one of Redwing Mine's revered Artisans, in fact one of the Province's most sought after journeyperson.

There was nothing to show that I once occupied a medium density house that I had fully furnished with state of the art furniture. There was nothing to show that not long ago, I used to drink and eat from some of Mutare's top notch joints and hotels.

There was nothing to show that my two wives Daisy and Diana were once envied tertiary students who had brighter futures. There was nothing to show that Daisy and Diana were once belles in their own right, belles who had swept me off my feet.

There was nothing to suggest that Daisy and Diana's shrivelled and unbrasiered breasts were once firm, full, plumb, enticing to the lustful eye and soft to the touch like a parrot's breast.

There was nothing to suggest that I had on times without number fondled and suckled those breasts with gusto and verve.

I could no longer imagine myself suckling at them for the mere sight would sent a rush of bile into my mouth. We no longer took our baths as regularly and frequently as we used to do. We no longer valued ourselves.

All we cared about were the issues of bread and butter. We would go into the forest, chop some firewood, tie them into portable bundles, which we would hawk into Dangamvura for a living.

I would limp and push wheelbarrows of firewood into Dangamvura for hawking. Dangamvura residents would buy my firewood not out of need, but more out of sympathy for my status. I would bravely defy my status. Disability does not mean inability. I had to ride on that sympathy for survival whilst deep down I burnt with stigma. I was not born like that.

With my family's life continuing to sink into an abyss of poverty under the weight of inflation, I resolved to migrate to Botswana in an attempt to escape from the clutches of poverty that had kept me under siege since childhood.

Indeed, poverty ran deep in my family. It was like a generational, generic curse, a curse that I had inherited from my ancestors.

Staying in a foreign land where the language was foreign and the hosts' alien, aggressive and arrogant was really a tall order. Life would have been made easier had I been in the company and comfort of my wives. I was far from my people. I missed parental love. I longed for my wives' love and affection. I yearned for my conjugal rights. I had learnt the hard way that living in a foreign land away from Amai was really difficult.

CHAPTER 28

SEA OF POVERTY

I had to travel from Mutare, Bulawayo, Francistown and Gaborone by train. I was armed with a myriad of mobile contacts who I intended to get in touch once I arrived in Gaborone.

Unfortunately, I failed to link up with a number of my *friends* in Botswana. Some of these *friends* of mine had pledged to cater for my needs should I decide to migrate to that country.

Others had promised to assist me to secure employment with their vast connections in Botswana upon my arrival.

But alas when I finally arrived in Gabs, the bulk of these *friends* of mine and acquaintances switched off their mobile phones whilst a few had the audacity of lying about their whereabouts. Some claimed to have been working out of Gabs and would only be back after a few months.

Others advised me to look for accommodation and jobs that they had claimed were abound, just to lure him into a sea of poverty.

One childhood friend of mine who resided in Gaborone's Mogoditsane, I had tried to contact had resorted to answering my calls in seTswana which I was not conversant in, just to give the impression that I had connected to a wrong subscriber. The other one from my hood in Dangamvura, Mutare, had told me directly that there was no way he could accommodate him since his lodgings were only meant for his wife, three kids and him.

But this was the same guy who had been bragging about his exploits in Botswana. He was the very guy who had told everyone within earshot how successful he had been in Botswana.

This was the same fellow who had bragged about the expensive and spacious house he had built and completed in Phakhalane suburb as well as top of the range vehicles that he had added to his vast empire.

This was the guy who claimed to have been connected to Botswana's business moguls. He was the guy who claimed to have been sitting in a number of boards in companies that were listed on the Botswana Stock Exchange.

Upon arrival in Molepolole, I was astounded to find hordes of

Zimbabweans lining up a street near the rank where they touted for menial jobs.

Most Zimbabweans then stayed at a house near the rank that was owned by a Zimbabwean man, a Madyirapazhe.

Along the road near the rank that had become an employment centre, I had linked up with Dafi, The Bull Frog a renowned martial artiste and an old schoolmate from Dangamvura High School, who took me in his grass-thatched hut. A hut that leaked like a sieve during the rainy season. We had no pots with us and survived on bread and sweet drinks, Jolly Juices or Davitas. After a week, we began to feel the ripple effects of a lack our staple food, sadza. I had failed to travel to Gaborone for days.

Fortunately, a Zimbabwean couple came to our aid by offering us sadza and mufushwa wemunyemba known as *motsogo*, which was mixed with makanda ehuku. We ate until we were left waddling in puddles of sweat. We had survived to tell tales of another day.

I can vividly recall that black Friday of 26 November 2006. It was black in the sense that, the following day saw me becoming an illegal immigrant or *chinyau* in the migration parlance. I had failed to travel to Gaborone for day's extension due to financial constraints.

I had failed to land any job having crossed into that country via Ramokgwabana rail border post. At Khama Khama's makeshift house that was still under construction, I had witnessed all sorts of social vices. Some married women engaged in adulterous affairs with fellow Zimbabweans.

I had witnessed some Zimbabwean prostitutes getting into sexual orgies just behind Khama Khama's Blair toilet, all under the cover of darkness and intoxicating substances.

I had witnessed a number of catfights that regularly broke out among Zimbabwean prostitutes who would be battling for clients.

I had sadly witnessed some Zimbabwean shoplifters, illegal immigrants and muggers being nabbed by the police in pre-dawn raids.

I had also seen some unscrupulous Zimbabweans mastering the art of evading or rather systematically avoiding paying their daily rentals to Khama Khama by trooping home in the wee hours and sneaking away before the crack of dawn.

After failing to secure any form of employment and almost on the verge of bankruptcy, I resolved to relocate to Molepolole village, which is about 15kms from Gabs.

Some Zimbabweans who I had met at White City, a diamond sorting centre in Gaborone, had hinted that I might land a job on the farms since Molepolole was close to several cattle posts and farms.

CHAPTER 29

A heavy knock thundered on the dilapidated door of my ramshackle lodgings that was under termite siege. When the second knock rattled against the makeshift door threatening to rip it from her hinges, I shot out of a tattered sleeping bag, as if from a catapult.

I had just not emerged from a nightmare. This was real. The knock that had jerked me into life had been delivered by Tatenda Moyondizvo who had come to warn me of a looming crackdown that was to be carried out by the Botswana Police, Army, the notorious Special Service Group, SSG and the immigration arm on all illegal foreigners who roamed the streets of Molepolole.

The previous raid effected at the crack of dawn in the same village, had netted in hundreds of illegal Zimbabwean immigrants.

A good number of Zimbabweans who had decided or rather chosen to stay in Botswana illegally, had been swooped upon across the country and were awaiting deportation aboard immigration trucks, *magumba kumba*.

Those Zimbos were being detained across the windswept nation. Moyondizvo and I stealthily wormed our way into a nearby thick bush where we sought sanctuary among some slithering reptiles and stinging scorpions.

Having stashed away a few supplies of food among some Mopani bushes, we drifted into horror land. We slept horribly, dreamt horrors as we took a trip down a nocturnal lane of horrendous flutter of eyes that were heavy with horrors.

Two days later, when the raids were officially called off, we landed a six-day contract with a Motswana who was notoriously referred to by Zimbabweans as Muchademba meaning you shall regret.

Muchademba, who was known among his compatriots as Ra Mosimane or Shalala, had gained notoriety among Zimbabweans for his unorthodox means of acquiring cheap labour force whose services mostly were mostly rendered for *free*.

Shalala would level a myriad of trumped up charges against Zimbabweans who he would have hired for months on end without their wages, if they dared to ask for their dues. After securing the six-day contract through Mudhara Shumbayaonda of Mufakose, my nineteen compatriots and I boarded Shalala's haulage truck that was being driven by Mhlanga from Chipinge.

All in all, we were twenty Zimbabweans who were aboard that haulage truck. Among us were Mudhara Shumbayaonda who had been appointed manager because of his advanced age, martial arts and special constabulary background back at home.

Mhlanga the haulage truck driver, Malayitsha a class four driver from Magwegwe, Bulawayo and two females Rudorwashe and Mutsawashe who had been hired as cooks for us travelled in the haulage truck.

Meanwhile, the haulage truck that transported us developed a mechanical fault, sauntered, spurted, splintered coughed, spit and threw up to a halt along the highway to Sojwe.

Efforts to resuscitate the truck that did not appear decimated, rickety, malnourished and pale were fruitless. Efforts to try to mend the haulage truck that resembled a gliding millipede were tantamount to flogging a dead mule. We had to sleep huddled around a dying fire since some of us were not in possession of blankets.

We had to take turns to rekindle the dying fire that was fired with some thorn shrubs. Temperatures had fallen since the country had been pounded and pummelled with a heavy down pour punctuated with some light hailstones.

We had to sleep on empty stomachs since Ra Mosimane had taken our food rations ahead with him.

The following morning, the mechanical fault was rectified and we resumed with our journey.

In Sojwe, *the cattle recovery or loss control team* set about recapturing beasts that had gone astray. Later, we were driven to one of Ra Mosimane's five cattle posts in Gbabadju where lions prowled during the night in search of water from water troughs.

Lions would prowl around the farm's makeshift farm tin-house. A few days later, we were driven through Kalahari Desert to Zintshantshi where were set about repairing a broken down fence. The six-day contract melted into weeks and later months, which were all not paid for.

Whenever Ra Mosimane realised that disgruntlement among his Zimbabwean labourers was running high, he would visit all the farms manned by Zimbabweans collecting cattle, which he would sell to the Botswana Meat Company, BMC.

He would promise to service all wage debts he owed his workers that would lift morale among his employees that would have plunged to an all-time low.

I kept my hair unkempt, sported dreadlocks, imbibed the traditional brew Khadi, smoked mbanje, *mothokwani* and got hooked to Basarwa girls.

As frustration took its toll on me, I would ride to Diphuduhudu on Shalala's horse where I had found love in a Basarwa lady. By then, I was a hard-core illegal immigrant. Myths are abound about this Basarwa tribe, which is accused of all sorts of social vices and etiquettes. Tradition has it that the Basarwa do not bath, but simply smear their bodies with ashes to keep away odours.

As I prepared to ride to Diphuduhudu to visit my girlfriend, five cattle from a nearby farm broke into Shalala's kraal in search of water. I was riled by that incident that nearly scuttled my journey to Diphuduhudu. I could not get down to mend the fence as that would have prevented me from visiting my girlfriend. I herded the cattle into a crush or loading pen where I secured them in intending to call the owner the following morning with a view to make him repair the kraal.

Having been satisfied with the measures I had taken, I galloped to Diphuduhudu on Ra Mosimane's horse.

After arriving in Diphuduhudu where I had taken along madila, sour milk that would have been compacted by hanging it out in a sack leaving only solidified creamy milk that can be consumed with meat, for my girlfriend. I relaxed at my girlfriend's place enjoying a dish of madila and magwinya.

In the middle of the night as I snored away exhausted and clasped in the arms of my girlfriend, a heavy knock pounded a ramshackle door to a dilapidated shack that served as our bedroom.

I later learnt that a rival suitor, a Mosarwa who claimed to have spent a fortune on the two timing girlfriend was seething with anger threatening to stab me with a knife, *tipha* or worse still set the hut in which we were sleeping ablaze.

My rival suitor had unleashed my boss, lekhuwa's horse, in a bid to foil my bid for a good escape.

I swiftly dressed up, picked up an axe, and stormed out

brandishing it into the face of my rival who took to flight, as he feared for his life.

I went to where I had tied the horse, but it was nowhere in sight. It was at that juncture that I knew that my rival had set it free. I searched for the animal under moonlight. Fortunately, when I found the horse, my rival who had gone out to look for reinforcements was still to close in on me.

CHAPTER 30

UNDER CORDON

I was under siege. I mounted the horse and spurred the animal through a human barrier, sending the barricaders scurrying for cover. When I arrived home, I panted into the temporary farm hut where I slept under a palpitating heart until daybreak.

I got the shock of my life when I discovered that three of the five cattle I had secured in a crash pen had died due to stampeding. I informed the owner who came to collect the carcases.

The owner appeared to have understood the circumstances surrounding the demise of his animals and had accepted the situation.

He later somersaulted his mind after being pressured by his compatriots who wanted him to lay charges against me, a mere poor Zimbabwean cattle herder. Police officers picked me up from Sojwe where a myriad of charges were preferred against me.

I was later hauled before a chief's court, *kgotha* where I was found guilty of cattle slaughter, over-staying as well as working without a work permit.

There I was sentenced to three strokes, which left some indelible marks on my backside as well as excruciating pain. There at the kgotha, I shed tears of migration. There in the cells at Sojwe where I was a lone inmate for five days, I nursed my scars of migration and shed tears of migration.

There at Sojwe police cells I was to re-unite with Tichaendepi from Chegutu farms. Tichaendepi who prior to his migrating to Botswana had been a devout member of the Johane Marange apostolic sect, had been nabbed by police at Zintshatshi cattle post where he had been posted as my replacement.

We had separated when he was posted to Kgatswane cattle post. He had not been paid since we were engaged for a six-day fence re-pairing contract.

He had been moved from one cattle post to another. On May Day, the day he was arrested, he had just returned from the kraal where he had been milking in readiness for breakfast.

He had a premonition that something sinister was going to take place that day. Around mid-day, Tichaendepi had arrived from the kraal carrying a 20Litre bucket of *maswi*, milk.

He had just placed the pail of *maswi*, sneaked into the makeshift tinned house to rest on a temporary bed when he heard the sound of a police Land Cruiser roaring into the cattle post.

Before he could take any action, the Land Cruiser had screeched to a cruising halt sending a cloud of dust into the air, a cloud that left Tichaendepi blinded and tearful.

With the blink of an eye, two police officers leapt out of the police marked Land Cruiser and strode towards a bemused Tichaendepi who remained transfixed to the spot like a cockroach that had been paralysed and hypotenused with the effects of Baygon.

'*Dumela Ra, lekhayi, litsukhile, lekhayi,*' one of the policemen had greeted him in the deep Setswana accent.

'*Lethenghi Ra, litsukhile,*' Tichaendepi had answered.

'Hey man, *phambili ikhayi?*

Tichaendepi still gripped with fear, jack kneed into the makeshift shelter that he had called home to fish out his passport. Having fished the passport from the dusty homemade bed, he had handed it over to one of the officers. '*Phambili kheone Ra, tsa!*'

After perusing through the travelling document, the officer had asked, '*Hey mna, malatse akhayi?*

'*Malatsehaayo Ra, aphedile,*' Tichaendepi had replied.

'Man get into the truck, let's go. Be quick time is flying,' the officer had grunted

Tichaendepi had got into the tinned shelter, stuffed a tattered and threadbare Ra Maswabi's blanket that he had been using into an empty maize-meal sack before storming into the back of the Cruiser, which cruised him through a stretch of cattle posts to Sojwe.

At Sojwe, I was re-united with Tichaendepi my compatriot. That brought to two, the number of inmates at Sojwe holding cells. Tichaendepi had tearfully narrated to me the reason behind his migration to Botswana.

Tichaendepi had grown up in a polygamous family set-up in Chegutu where his father owned a farm. After dropping out of school in Form Three due to a myriad of financial hiccups, Tichaendepi had migrated to Harare where he had stayed with a distant maternal uncle who ran a security firm.

The uncle had swiftly offered him employment as a sentinel. He was assigned to guard a boutique in the city centre. During the course of his employment, he connived to siphon goods with the manager of the boutique.

When the crime was detected, Tichaendepi was picked up for interrogation as a first suspect. During the process, he owned up and implicated the manager leading to his subsequent arrest.

Tichaendepi skipped the country into Botswana after he was granted bail. The courts had failed to realise that Tichaendepi could be a flight risk.

The conventional court in Gaborone slapped me with an effective three months' sentence after I pleaded guilty to causing the death of three beats. I did my time in a Gaborone prison.

Upon my release from prison, Ra Mosimane who had never paid me a single visit, tried to bribe immigration officers not to deport me and instead release me into his hands, for he reckoned I was an industrious and honest worker.

Ra Mosimane could not pay me even a single thebe claiming he was in the red. Thebe was the smallest denomination of the Botswana currency. I was deported with nothing to show for my toil as I had not been paid by Ra Mosimane.

I had been used and later discarded like a pair of worn out socks. As if that was not enough, I had lost all my clothes to fellow deportees.

After being surrendered to Zimbabwean immigration authorities at Plumtree border post, I had to hatch a plan to sneak back into Botswana where I intended to confront Ra Mosimane with the sole aim of recouping my dues. I had been toughened by my stint in prison.

Life in prison and worse still a foreign prison, had stirred the monster that had been lurking in me. I was an ex-convict who had served time in a prison where I had mixed and mingled with convicts who were doing time for a litany of criminal offences.

My stint in that Gaborone jail, stirred the xenophobia demon that had been lying dormant in me for years. I then hated Batswanas with a passion.

I loathed Ra Mosimane with a burning passion for he had never bothered to pay me a single visit during my three months' stint or made any attempts to attend the trial that led to my conviction. I still felt Ra Mosimane should have been arraigned before the courts for having employed me fully knowing that I was an illegal immigrant who did not possess a work permit.

He knew he was committing an offence and should have been arrested for collusion. He got away with *murder* because he knew how to sweet talk his compatriots. He was riding on lady luck coupled with a system that treated foreigners as worse off than animals.

I sneaked into Botswana. I had to skirt Ramokgwabana border post as the sun was about to retreat into her shell with the eventful day in tow.

Chapter 31

The Fugitive

However, I ran out of luck before I had made any meaningful progress and was captured like a fugitive from justice. I was bundled into a police Land Cruiser together with a female compatriot who had been nabbed for trying to cross into that country illegally.

The woman who I later came to know as Raviro, had resorted to illegal means of migration after her estranged husband had walked out on her. The police who had been outwitted by a Zimbabwean cigarette smuggler who had left behind his contraband, were determined to vent off their anger by pressing some smuggling charges against the hapless Raviro

I impressed upon Raviro who by then was weeping uncontrollably, on the need to escape from lawful custody as soon as the Cruiser slowed down to negotiate a corner.

At first, she was against the idea, but when I enlightened her on the gravity of the crime she was facing, she resolved to play ball.

As fate would have it, the Cruiser slowed down almost to a screeching halt allowing us to parachute onto the tarmac like stuntmen. We rolled onto the tarmac with our loot from the contraband, which we intended to hawk for our transport fares to Francistown and train fares to Gaborone. Having recovered from the numbness brought by the impact of gravitational fall, we flagged down a lift to Francistown where we hawked our loot whose proceeds we used to pay for train fares to Gaborone. We later separated in Gaborone as I boarded a Molepolole bound coach. I checked Ra Mosimane at his home, but was told that he had visited his Mahukhutswane cattle post.

Ra Mosimane was elated to see me and he quickly made his intentions of reengaging me known, but I declined, as I wanted my dues to be paid first. I stayed at the cattle post where a number of Zimbabweans had been hired to perform a plethora of tasks.

With no payment of mine dues in sight, and disgruntled as I was, I incited my compatriots to embark on an industrial action. Ra Mosimane tabled three options for me.

I was supposed to either resume work, face deportation or

eviction. Under siege, I buckled in, resumed duties and got posted to Gbabadju where lions roared and prowled in the dead of the night.

I resumed work at the end of August 2007 and laboured up to November of the same year without being paid a single thebe. I almost got tempted to sell off all calves that were born during Ra Mosimane's absence, but I feared for the worst. Ra Mosimane was notorious for spending a sizeable chunk of his fortune on traditional healers from Zambia and Zimbabwe even though he claimed to be a devout born again Christian.

CHAPTER 32

THE IRRESISTIBLE INTRUDER

I woke up with a start, the same start that you would have if you were to wake up in a mortuary surrounded by an army of rambling corpses.

Beads of sweat had formed on my face and cascading down my face. I had just awoken from an outlandish that had left me energy burrowed. I could see some streaks of moonlight streaming into my tumble down servants quarters whose door was under termite cordon and perilously hanging by a thread.

As I fumbled to my left side, I caressed a female breast, which was plump and cupped in a velvet skin that was as soft as an impressionist's breast.

I was taken aback by the new twist of events. An intruder had slipped into my blankets. Blankets that had seen better days.

Blankets that leaked like a sieve. Blankets that enabled me to see through the moon. Blankets that were fortunate to be held together by a string of fatigued and threadbare seams.

An irresistible intruder slept soundly beside me. Her arms were passionately thrown around me, astounded as I was. My heart was then palpitating heavily, threatening to tear the rib cage into smithereens. I just could not fathom the events of the previous night. It appeared I was under the influence of a drug of some sort. When I finally recollected from my whirlwind of senses, I realised that I had sampled Ra Mosimane's jealously guarded honey pot.

I had sexually satisfied my sexually starved fearsome Master's wife who had blackmailed me into making love to her the previous night. Madam Lebone had used unorthodox means to lure me to bed by drugging me with a concoction that was laced with some aphrodisiacs as she sought to abuse me sexually. I was only thirty-two whilst Madam Lebone, a light skinned lady of rare beauty, was twenty years my senior.

Despite her age, she was still as attractive as a teenager. For the past three months or so she had desperately tried to entice me to her matrimonial bedroom but to no avail.

For the past few months that I had been under the employment of the Mosimanes, Ma Lebone, a unique light as her name suggested, had tried unsuccessful to lure me to her matrimonial bed.

Not once, not twice but thrice, she had stormed into my makeshift bathroom as I bathed at the cattle post where she usually visited whenever her husband would have travelled to South Africa for business.

On all those occasions, she had been dressed in a skimpy and too revealing romantic nightgown that left nothing to the imagination. On all those occasions, Ma Lebone had romantically caressed my manhood which she had glowingly sang praises of as she drew lines of comparisons between it and that boyish tiny thing of her *useless in bed husband.*

Thrice she almost successfully forced herself on me despite my handicap. Thrice I had left the passionate struck Ma Lebone groaning, moaning and clutching to her boobs with mouth ajar.

That previous night, I had just arrived from my cattle post to collect my meagre wages. Nobody was home save for Ma Lebone.

Her husband had travelled to South Africa and would not be back that night whilst their three children were all attending school in Canada.

When I knocked on the door to the main house, she had shouted from the bathroom in Setswana, 'Khemani?'

'Khena Ma,' I had responded.

'Hey Bantu bamodimo, wena mosimane hauna lena?' She had shouted back.

'Khena Jo Ma,'

'Tsena monto mosimane, khiyetha, nakhiyathapha,' I was told to enter.

Five minutes later, Ma Lebone had strode out of the bathroom, fresh, dripping with wetness and stark naked. She had unashamedly and ungracefully ambled her way towards me. I was struck with awe and bewilderment. There she was Ma Lebone, crafted to perfection. I was perplexed, thunderstruck and held spellbound by the beauty queen. I had remained transfixed to the seat, drooling and salivating with lust.

Ma Lebone had made her statement and the effect was already telling or rather showing on me.

My eyes had remained glued on her attractive body, my eyes threatening to pop out of their sockets. Never in my life had I seen a lady as beautiful as Ma Lebone, not even in Mutare where I was raised.

She had embraced me and before I could recollect, Ma Lebone started to kiss me passionately whilst at the same time working into my pant, arousing my anaconda into a striking position.

I had been swept away from my pedestal, had drifted into a dreamland that had left me with more dreams than those I could accommodate in my land of dreams, the dreamland, an abyss of dreams, an oasis of dreams that left me in bated breath.

As I desperately tried to come to terms with events of the previous night, a heavy knock thundered on my derelict door hounding to rip it from its hinges. Before I could attend to the knock, startled as I was, the person behind the knock bulldozed into the gloomy room that resembled a dungeon of despair.

I could tell from the silhouette figure that it was my boss lekhuwa Ra Mosimane who had groped his way into the filth and smelly dilapidated dungeon of room that was adjacent to a fowl run that housed several chickens.

It was the smell of chicken droppings that permeated through my quarters. Any visitor could be forgiven for thinking that I lived in a fowl run for foul smell from chicken droppings ran through thick and fast. The foul smell from chicken droppings had literally taken over my quarters, the pong from the birds' droppings had literally invaded the dungeon.

A light from his torch beam, confirmed my worst fears. We had been caught in the act, caught red handed, caught with incriminating evidence by an ex-convict and murderer who had served time for axing his wife's boyfriend. *Could I be the next victim?*

Could my name be added to statistics of crimes of passion? I wondered. When my lekhuwa realised that his wife had leased his honey pot to their ragged servant, me, he slumped to the floor, sending the torch clattering to the floor. He had passed out.

The reality of the event was too amorous, too explicit, too revealing and just too painful to sink in. The two of us, oblivious of the fact that we were still in our birthday suits, sounded some piercing distress calls that sliced through the night. In no time, some *badisa badikgomo*, cattle herders from nearby cattle posts responded to our distress calls. They were bemused by what they had seen.

Both the respectable Ma Lebone and I were stark naked and

never made any efforts to cover our nudity as we desperately tried to resuscitate Ra Mosimane.

Ra Mosimane was finally bundled into his car as Ma Lebone and I simply covered our nakedness with our clothes that had been lying strewn on the dirty floor.

As Ma Lebone cruised through cattle posts to Dhiphuduhudu Clinic where she intended to take her husband, her mind was racing.

I was shaking uncontrollably and drenched to the bone under a deluge of sweat. I developed butterflies in my stomach. I ended up nearly soiling myself.

I could not imagine myself facing Ra Mosimane should he regain consciousness, after my carnal knowledge with Ma Lebone. Ma Lebone who was blaming herself for the mess we were in, angrily brought the car to a halt.

I had resolved to run away as I feared for the worst at the hands of Ra Mosimane who had once brandished and trained a gun at me when twenty of his cattle had strayed out from the farm some time back.

I vividly recalled how Ma Lebone had come to my rescue. I weaved my way into the gloomy forest and in no time, had been swallowed by the forest that appeared to offer me a temporary sanctuary and relief.

CHAPTER 33

DUNGEON OF SANCTUARY

Unbeknown to me, Ma Lebone had also resolved to trail me into that thick dungeon of a forest. I was jerked into a reality check by well-manicured and dainty hands that tapped onto my shoulder, hands that still reeked with odours associated with a lascivious act.

An amateur punch aimed at my goatee bearded handsome face, knocked me off balance sending me sprawling into the cold fine sand soil. Blood gushed from my mouth as if from a fireman's canon.

'Where do you think you are going mosimane, we are in this together mosimane? I really love you and will not just let you go especially after the mess that we are in. 'Let's face the music as adults. Let's deal with the problem at hand first and see how things pan out,' said Ma Lebone angrily whilst panting for breath.

I picked myself up, dusted myself and spit a mouthful of blood onto the soil. Ma Lebone grabbed me by the belt and led me back to the car where Ra Mosimane lay unconscious.

She opened the door to the passenger seat and threw me into the car, which squeaked as if in protest. She got behind the wheel and ploughed through waves of sandy dunes leaving behind a cloud of dust and furrow like marks on the sandy road. When we finally arrived at Diphuduhudu, Ra Mosimane had regained consciousness, but was still dazzled to act. He was attended to and admitted as medical personnel there intended to monitor his progress overnight. After being assured by the medical team that Ra Mosimane who was asthmatic as well as diabetic was out of danger as he had responded to treatment, Ma Lebone and I drove back to the cattle post.

Whilst at the cattle post, we resolved to flee to Zimbabwe as we feared that Ra Mosimane would be out to even scores. He had once served time for killing a man who he had stumbled upon bedding the voluptuous and vivacious Ma Lebone.

The unpredictable and temperamental Ra Mosimane had once been incarcerated for a decade after being convicted of passionate killing and chances of him killing again were very high.

I packed my tattered clothes, clothes that had seen better days into a mealie-meal empty bag that had served me so well in Botswana as my bag. I had also packed a threadbare blanket.

Ma Lebone threw my possessions back into the decrepit quarters and advised me to carry only my passport. She reckoned that being in possession of such clothes, clothes that reeked with abject poverty, would give me away to law enforcement agents and immigration officers. We drove to Molepolole where Ma Lebone packed her clothes and travelling documents. She bought me a new wardrobe of clothes that befitted her status.

From there, we drove to Sojwe enroute to Francistown via Serowe, the land of salt, letswai. In Francis Town, she withdrew large sums of money, transferred a large chunk of the family fortune into a new Zimbabwean bank account after which we drove to border Ramokgwabane near Plumtree. After being given the all clear into Zimbabwe, we shed tears. Tears of joy, joy that we were finally safe from the vengeful Ra Mosimane. We shed tears of guilt, guilt that we had robbed a hardworking man of his fortune. I had had my sweet revenge.

Meanwhile, when news of Ma Lebone and my flight to Zimbabwe got to Ra Mosimane as he recuperated in an upmarket private hospital in Gaborone where he had been airlifted to, he knew his world had crumpled around him.

He just could not believe that he had lost his wife of twenty years to a mere cattle herder from Zimbabwe, *modisa wa digkomo*. No amount of explanation could make him believe that I had been drugged into engaging in those sexual acts. Frothing at the mouth, he had sworn that he would not rest until he had killed the two of us. He had vowed to hunt us down for having betrayed and abandoned him to die in a remote hospital.

www.ingramcontent.com/pod-product-compliance
Lightning Source LLC
Chambersburg PA
CBHW031842170626
46807CB00004B/1589